Reflective Learning in Management, Development and Education

In recent years there has been a growing interest in the ideas surrounding reflective practice, specifically in the areas of learning in management, development and education. This interest has developed in a growing number of professional fields thus making for very diverse understandings of what can be regarded as complex approaches to learning.

In order to understand how reflective practice can support and aid learning it is helpful to acknowledge how we learn. First, all learners start from their own position of knowledge and have their own set of experiences to draw upon. Second, learning is contextual, something which managers need to acknowledge. To make sense and achieve a deep understanding of material and experiences, one needs to relate new information to existing knowledge and experiences. This is best achieved through a process of reflection. Indeed, the underlying rationale for the chapters in this book is to explore how the role of practice, reflection and critical reflection are understood and developed within a learning process which is supported through the application of reflective tools.

This book recognises and makes explicit the diverse, yet inclusive, nature of the field. By including a range of contributions from both subject specific disciplines and professional contexts, it seeks to enable the reader in documenting some of the current uses of reflection and critical reflection, while also illustrating some of the newer methods in use, as well as the current contributions to thinking in the subject domain. Through this book the editor and authors hope to provide a basis from which continuing professional development and education can be enhanced.

This book was originally published as a special issue of *Reflective Practice: International and Multidisciplinary Perspectives*.

David Higgins is currently a Senior Lecturer in organisational behaviour/management at the University of Huddersfield, UK. During the last seven years he has developed as an accomplished researcher and academic; he has written to date a number of peer reviewed articles/conference papers on the mediated nature of practice-based learning and social learning in the small firm. He has been the recipient of three ESRC Research Bursaries Awards, is currently a reviewer for the *World Conference on Small Business and Entrepreneurship* and the *Institute of Small Business and Enterprise*. He is a fellow of the HEA and a member of BAM Research Methods SIG. David's research interest focuses on the current conceptualisations of learning in the small firm.

Reflective Learning in Management, Development and Education

Edited by
David Higgins

Routledge
Taylor & Francis Group

LONDON AND NEW YORK

First published 2014
by Routledge
2 Park Square, Milton Park, Abingdon, Oxon, OX14 4RN

Simultaneously published in the USA and Canada
by Routledge
711 Third Avenue, New York, NY 10017

Routledge is an imprint of the Taylor & Francis Group, an informa business

© 2014 Taylor & Francis

British Library Cataloguing in Publication Data
A catalogue record for this book is available from the British Library

ISBN13: 978-0-415-70442-7

Typeset in Times New Roman
by Taylor & Francis Books

Publisher's Note
The publisher accepts responsibility for any inconsistencies that may have arisen during the conversion of this book from journal articles to book chapters, namely the possible inclusion of journal terminology.

Disclaimer
Every effort has been made to contact copyright holders for their permission to reprint material in this book. The publishers would be grateful to hear from any copyright holder who is not here acknowledged and will undertake to rectify any errors or omissions in future editions of this book.

Contents

Citation Information

The chapters in this book were originally published in *Reflective Practice: International and Multidisciplinary Perspectives*, volume 12, issue 5 (October 2011). When citing this material, please use the original page numbering for each article, as follows:

Chapter 6

Advancement of guided creative and critical reflection in the professional development of enterprising individuals in business and nursing
Ruth Anne Fraser and Jasna K. Schwind
Reflective Practice: International and Multidisciplinary Perspectives, volume 12, issue 5 (October 2011) pp. 645–661

Chapter 7

Reflective Learning and Clerical staff at a University College in the Cayman Islands: Implications for Management (An Exploratory Study)
Mark A. Minott, Allan E. Young and Carolyn Mathews
Reflective Practice: International and Multidisciplinary Perspectives, volume 12, issue 5 (October 2011) pp. 663–677

Chapter 8

Wikis: building a learning experience between academe and businesses
Keith Halcro and Anne M.J. Smith
Reflective Practice: International and Multidisciplinary Perspectives, volume 12, issue 5 (October 2011) pp. 679–693

Notes on Contributors

Yngve Antonsen has a PhD from the University of Tromsø, Norway. His research focuses on management and learning in organisations. He has published chapters in edited books and articles in the *Journal of Workplace Learning*. Previously he worked as an Assistant Professor in the field of adult education and competence development at the University of Tromsø, Norway.

Rosemary Athayde is a Senior Researcher/Lecturer at the Small Business Research Centre at Kingston University, UK, and is involved in a wide range of projects, including a project for Business Link London, and an Equality and Human Rights Commission-funded project investigating the procurement policies and practices of the Olympic Delivery Authority for the 2012 London Olympic Games. She has carried out evaluations of different types of enterprise education programmes using a range of psychometric measures and techniques.

Elizabeth Chell, PhD, FRSA, FBAM, retired from a full-time academic career in 2007 and now operates on a part-time basis as Professor of Entrepreneurial Behaviour and research consultant in the Small Business Research Centre at Kingston University, UK. Since 1991 she has held chairs as a full Professor at the universities of Southampton, UMIST, and Newcastle. Her current responsibilities focus on research and publishing. She is a fellow of the Royal Society for the Arts, Manufactures and Commerce and the British Academy of Management. Elizabeth was recently appointed to the CMI Academic Advisory Committee.

Jonathan Deacon is a Reader in Marketing and Entrepreneurship at Newport Business, University of Wales, Newport, UK.

Ruth Anne Fraser, PhD, is President and sole owner of Fraser Education, Uxbridge, Canada, and provides career and professional development support to business workers, educators and students. In these contexts, Anne's research, professional development, curriculum development, coaching and workshops include participants' lived experiences, which have potential for insight into improved practice and worker satisfaction.

Keith Halcro is a Senior Lecturer in Strategy and Innovation at Glasgow Caledonian University, UK. His research interests lie in innovation within rural and social enterprises/museums, particularly in relation to strategic management and the idea of competitive advantage.

Jacqueline Harris is a Senior Lecturer in Marketing at Newport Business, University of Wales, Newport, UK.

Carolyn Mathews is a Professor and Chair of Graduate Studies and Executive Training at the University College of the Cayman Islands. Her research interests include human resource management, professionalism, creative curriculum design in academic contexts and applied research especially in the context of human resource management. Recent research includes: an evaluation of the Jury Education Induction Program in South Australia commissioned by the South Australian Law Society; researching the mental health of children in primary schools, commissioned by the Australian College of Educators; and the development of a set of guiding principles designed to shape the development of bushfire education programmes in South Australia, commissioned by the South Australian County Fire Service (CFS).

Mark A. Minott is an Associate Professor in the Department of Teacher Education at the University College of the Cayman Islands. His research interests include teacher education, reflective teaching, ICT in the classroom and the arts in education. His writings are found in journals such as *Reflective Practice: Multidisciplinary Perspectives* (UK), *Australian Journal of Teacher Education*, *Professional Development in Education* (UK), *Current Issues in Education* (USA), *International Journal of Music Education* (UK), *College Quarterly* (Canada), *Journal of the University College of the Cayman Islands* and the *Journal for Research on Christian Education* (USA). He is peer reviewer for a number of international journals. He is the author of *Reflective Teaching: Properties, Tool, Benefits and Support* and *Reflection and Reflective Teaching*: *A Case Study of Four Seasoned Teachers in the Cayman Islands*.

Scott Parfitt is a Senior Lecturer in Supply Chain Management at Glamorgan Business School, University of Glamorgan, UK. His research interests include category management in the public sector and small independent retailers.

Kath Ringwald is a Principal Lecturer in Supply Chain Management at Glamorgan Business School, University of Glamorgan, UK. Her research interests include SME engagement in public sector procurement, supplier relationships management and small independent retailers.

Jasna K. Schwind, PhD, is an Associate Professor in the Daphne Cockwell School of Nursing at Ryerson University, Toronto, Canada. Her programme of research focuses on reconstruction of the personal and professional self within therapeutic relationships in nursing education and practice. More specifically, using Narrative Inquiry, Jasna explores the humanness aspect of caregiver-carereceiver interactions and how these impact the quality of patients' illness experiences. Jasna has adapted a form of narrative reflection she terms Narrative Reflective Process (NRP) to use for both creative data collection and intervention purposes.

Anne M.J. Smith lectures in Entrepreneurship and Innovation at Glasgow Caledonian University, UK. Survival, success and growth of firms are the foundation of her research, which are interests derived from being third generation family business. Anne has successfully published articles in a range of international entrepreneurship journals covering enterprise education, learning and rural entrepreneurship.

Odd Arne Thunberg has a PhD from the University of Tromsø, Norway. He has published chapters in edited books and published articles in the *Journal of Workplace Learning*. Previously he worked as an Assistant Professor in the field of vocational learning at the University of Tromsø, Norway. He has also been director of the project Teacher Students as fellow Researchers and School Development Agents.

Tom Tiller is a Professor in the Department of Education at the University of Tromsø, Norway. Tiller has led and collaborated on a series of action research projects. His research area is connected to organisational, rural school and municipality development. He has written and edited around 40 books. Among those is *Action Research – A Nordic Perspective*. He has also published in the *Journal of Education for Teaching* and in the *Journal of Workplace Learning*.

Allan E. Young is Chair and Professor of Teacher Education in the Teacher Education Department, as well as Professor in the College of Business at the University College of the Cayman Islands. He sits on the council of chairs as a representative for his department and is actively involved in various college committees and heads the quality assurance and accreditation initiatives for the University College of the Cayman Islands. Dr Young's research agenda is broad-based and reflects a myriad of interests, which includes, but is not limited to, the following areas: distance education; hybrid instruction; technology effectiveness; accounting education; and other issues relating to teaching and teaching effectiveness. He serves on the editorial boards of the *Journal of the University College of the Cayman Islands* and the *Turkish Online Journal of Distance Education*. Additionally, he has acted as peer reviewer for several articles.

INTRODUCTION

Why reflect? Recognising the link between learning and reflection

A large amount of material has been written over the years on management development relating to the issues of learning, training, and education. This special issue moves beyond previous studies, by exploring rationales for a management development approach that focuses on the practices of reflective learning which are most effective for management development and education. The articles contained in this special issue have sought to explore the challenges and opportunities for expediting reflection, as a practice, in the development of managers, professionals and students within the business community. The term reflective practice conveys meanings that range from the questioning of presuppositions and assumptions, through to more explicit engagement in the process of critical and creative thinking in order to make connections between experience and learning in practice and practical action. The practices of reflection suggest a method of inquiry which is characterised by engagement, pondering alternatives, drawing inferences and taking diverse perspectives, especially in situations which are complex and novel, calling for situational awareness and understanding. The development of reflective practices for managerial development and learning programmes is underpinned by an ability and willingness to question and explore ways of acting and thinking as we engage in business activities. This process of reflecting for, in and on action, makes it possible to change our current understanding of action by framing the issue or encounter in a different or novel way, or by improvising on new ways to solve the issue at hand.

The term reflection could be considered as a representation of human consciousness. Reflection as process or act refers to the means by which the human mind has knowing of itself and its thinking. Such a process is deeply embedded in the continuous relationship between action and reflection. In this sense one can conceptualise reflection as the action of turning (back) or fixing the thoughts on some subject, in order to learn. In terms of management development and learning, as illustrated in all the articles presented in this special issue it is quite apparent that reflection is one of the most important building blocks and drivers of human learning.

The appeal of such thinking to the process of management development and learning is the linking of learning with action, which is in direct contrast to some traditional academic approaches where these are disconnected. This is a key theme in this special issue. The sense of closeness between problems, challenges and practicalities of business and education, against the opportunities which can be gained by learning in and through experience, has resulted in the current importance of experiential learning and reflective practices, particularly in management development and learning. The influence of these ideas is evidenced in the articles presented which illustrate situations where reflections, on differing educational and practical experiences, can be used to underpin attempts to improve practice.

The process of reflection is of critical importance in terms of management development as it allows one to critique taken-for-granted assumptions, in order to become more open to differing ways of inquiry, points of view opinions and behaviours. In this special issue, reflection is seen as much more than simply understanding. It involves the inclusion of a process into ones cognitive structures, relating these to other forms of experience and understanding. Management development and learning can be enhanced through the use of reflection by surfacing and critiquing tacit understanding or taken-for-granted mental structures. An important role of reflection then is that of reviewing practice, taking time to step back and to ponder the meaning of what has happened, the impact of it and the direction one is taking.

The use of reflective practices in management development and learning is appealing as it raises the likelihood of learning being relevant, particularly in the day to day practice of business, therefore situated and meaningful to those who engage in it. The challenge, in my view, for readers of the special edition and the wider field of academia in general, is the assumption that learning based on the systematic, rigorous and public reflection on experience, represents a fundamental change in emphasis in thinking about how people learn in particular business situations.

The role of this special issue is to both explore, challenge and offer opportunities for advancing the process of reflective practices in managerial development and learning. The issue presents to the reader a number of articles which integrate reflective practices into their work as researchers and practitioners within organization based development programmes, as well as contributing to research development. The issue represents value to those who are contemplating the use of reflection within managerial development and learning processes as well as to those who may be seeking to make sense of their own experiences. Taken together the articles are a celebration of not only new research agendas but some strong forward thinking about the use of reflective practices in this particular field.

David Higgins
University of Huddersfield

Is reflective practice the key to survival for small independent retailers? Evidence from South-East Wales

Kath Ringwald and Scott Parfitt

Glamorgan Business School, Pontypridd, UK

This article considers the role of reflective practice in the survival of small independent retailers (SIRs), based on case studies of SIRs in South Wales. The research suggests that there are four key factors which determine an SIR's individual competitive *footprint*: the ambition of the owner-manager; the appropriateness of the location; the firm's understanding of the market and the environment; and the ability to differentiate the product and service offering. The findings also suggest that each factor's performance is improved through the owner-manager's' reflective practice. The case studies show how owner-managers' active responses to critical reflection improves the performance of the firm and develops organisational learning.

Introduction

This article considers the role of reflective practice in the survival of small independent retailers (SIRs), given increasingly aggressive competition and changing customer expectations (Coca-Stefaniak, Parker, & Rees, 2010). In particular it considers the fate of the non-grocery SIRs that for decades were a feature of every British high street – men's and ladies' fashion stores, hairdressers, furniture stores, DIY and hardware suppliers, florists, etc.

Despite the rapid loss of SIRs in the 1970s and 1980s – businesses were being lost at a rate of up to 45 per day in the UK (Dawson, 1983) – very little research was being undertaken into why, or what could be done to support SIRs. Only 1% of articles published in the *International Journal of Retail and Distribution Management* during the 1980s and 1990s focused on SIRs or local retailing (Bennison, Warnaby, & Pal, 2010). Calls for government support also fell on deaf ears and government policy regarding local shopping provision remained 'confused in aim and implementation' (Dawson, 1983, p. 32). Since the 1990s the consequences of declining high streets in our towns and unsustainable village stores in rural locations have received political, public and academic attention (House of Commons All-Party Parliamentary Small Shops Group, 2006; National Retail Planning Forum [NRPF], 2004; Pioch & Byrom, 2004; Bennison, Clarke, & Pal, 2005).

It is now generally recognised that the continued presence of SIRs and local shopping provision (LSP) offers economic and social benefits to urban and rural communities (Coco-Stefaniak et al., 2010; Pioch & Byram, 2004). In economic terms, SIRs contribute to the local economy by employing local people, developing local supply chains, e.g. using a local accountant, buying stationery from a local supplier and paying local business rates, etc. The Local Multiplier 3 developed by the National Economic Foundation is used to calculate the impact a source of income (say, a local SIR) can have on the economy based on the way that money is spent and re-spent, making a greater impact than the total turnover of the business might suggest. In terms of social benefits, SIRs can provide a focus for the local community where an established local market can be identified, which in turn will attract other new SIRs. Local SIRs allow residents with limited mobility a degree of independence (Guy, 2010) and lowers carbon emissions by reducing the need for car journeys. SIRs can also add value for consumers by providing goods and services tailored to local needs.

However, like all small businesses, SIRs have been burdened by the costs associated with new legislation and regulation. They cannot compete with the scale economies achieved by the chain stores and multinationals, nor can they access comparable global supply chains. Independent high street stores have also been hit by the closure of stalwarts like Woolworths, leaving more units empty and making town centres less attractive to customers (Bennison et al., 2010). Although there have been some signs that consumers are rejecting the homogeneity of the shopping mall in favour of a more unique, independent offering (Elms, Canning, de Kervenoael, Whysall, & Hallsworth, 2010), the onset of recession saw the supermarkets, multinationals and discount stores regain customer loyalty. Coca-Stefaniak et al. (2010) also suggest that SIRs suffer because they have no collective voice to represent their interests and because owner-managers (OMs) of SIRs have not received appropriate management training.

Given these difficulties, coupled with the rise of internet shopping and the attraction of shopping locations that offer retail and entertainment opportunities at a single out-of-town location, it is not difficult to see why SIRs are fighting for survival. Yet, there are examples of thriving independent retailers in almost every community, so how do they survive when so many others fail? This study seeks to explain how and why reflective practice appears to be giving SIRs a greater chance of success in the most challenging of environments.

This research is based on five case studies of SIRs in South-East Wales, prepared between 2009 and 2010. For the purpose of this study South-East Wales is defined as the area of the M4 corridor bounded by the border with England to the east, Swansea to the west, Abergavenny to the north and the Bristol Channel to the south. The area contains the three largest cities in Wales. Cardiff is the capital city of the principality. It has a well-established city shopping centre with Victorian arcades, traditional shopping streets which are now pedestrianised and several large shopping centres all linked to provide an extensive and impressive shopping experience with numerous adjacent car parks. Cardiff benefits from being within easy reach of the entire South-East Wales region, being no more than one hour by car or train from the boundaries. Swansea and Newport are both well served with retail outlets of all kinds, but both cities have been affected more significantly by the recent recession than Cardiff. The remainder of the area is made up of fairly affluent rural areas in the east around Chepstow and the Vale of Glamorgan in the west. In the centre are the former industrial valleys which stretch from the coast to the edge of the Brecon Beacons in the north. The valleys areas have experienced high levels of unemployment since the 1970s, with a decline in retailing in the area over the same period. Many town centres are now in severe decline. Shoppers have become accustomed to travelling to one of the cities for major purchases, with other needs being met locally.

Research methodology

This exploratory qualitative research was originally inspired by the BBC television series 'Mary Queen of Shops'. The programme shows how retail consultant Mary Portas works with failing SIRs to turn their fortunes around by advising on business planning, strategy, marketing, store layout, décor, product offering and customer service. As module tutors for a retail and supply chain module for undergraduate students, we were looking for an exciting and challenging project for students, and this seemed a very suitable model. Groups of five to six students were required to identify a non-grocery SIR willing to engage in the project. We found SIRs were willing to participate because they had a genuine wish to help the students and were very interested in their findings. Unlike many other types of small and medium enterprise (SME), SIRs are an under-researched group and appeared to welcome the interest shown in their problems. The students all received a briefing from the module tutors at the outset of the exercise which encouraged students to conduct a SWOT analysis of the business, identifying the strengths and weaknesses in relation to product range, merchandising, customer satisfaction, marketing and promotion, store layout, location, market awareness, management and leadership skills, etc. They were also encouraged to analyse the OMs ability to identify and respond to opportunities and threats in their immediate environment. In particular, they were advised to consider the role of the OM and his/her contribution to the direction and success of the business. The groups were given six weeks to act as consultants to their chosen SIR, during which time they developed a trust-based relationship with the OMs which afforded them excellent access to information. They used semi-structured interviews with OMs, staff and customers. They also observed consumer behaviour within the store. Some of the groups visited competitor outlets for comparison purposes. The module tutors supervised the research throughout.

At the end of the period each group produced a report for the 'client' and presented their findings to their peer group and tutors. Students had the opportunity to discuss one another's case studies, at which point it became evident that a pattern was emerging from the SWOT analyses of each company. The discussions within the student group were observed by the tutors. We facilitated these discussions as a focus group, to elicit additional information which had been obtained in the course of the study but which had not featured in the final presentations. Four key factors appeared to be common to all of the case studies to a greater or lesser degree. In each case the presence or absence of these factors appeared to impact upon the relative success of the organisation. The key factors are:

- The ambition of the OM. The OM has personal ambitions as an entrepreneur and/or ambitions for the business to be the best, the most profitable or the customers' first choice. The ambitions need not extend to business growth, though that might be a consequence of the achievement of ambition. There is a considerable body of literature relating to entrepreneurial motivation and ambition, but second- and third-generation owner-managers in family businesses may not consider themselves to be entrepreneurs and therefore their personal motivations for themselves and the business may not be 'entrepreneurial' in the conventional sense.

- The location of the retail outlet. In this context the desirable location is considered to be a position which is close to the customers' desired location, but not necessarily close to competitors, large or small. Indeed, some of the owner-managers would deliberately avoid close proximity to big-store competitors, lest it highlight the differences in product range and price.
- The owner-manager's awareness of the market – particularly customers and competitors. Owner-managers need to be aware of customer needs and expectations, which evolve over time. The OMs need to understand their target market or market segment and the nature of competition in that segment. They also need to understand the business context in which they compete, e.g. political and environmental factors which might impact on the market.
- The differentiation of product or service offering. Big-store competitors tend to offer a homogenous product range in every shopping centre and mall in the country. SIRs have the opportunity to tailor the offering to the market segment and offer a range of additional services that chains and multiples cannot offer.

From the four dimensions above we were able to produce a 'competitive footprint' which illustrates the relative strength of each factor. The larger the 'footprint' the more resilient and successful the SIR appeared to be. This led us to consider what might determine these 'footprints'. We (the authors) followed up the group research with interviews to clarify the findings and gain additional information regarding the personal motivations and reflexivity of the owner-managers where necessary. The interviews revealed that some of the OMs were consciously engaged in reflective practice – evaluating their ability to 'read' the market, re-evaluating previous assumptions and recognising the difference between 'real' and 'perceived' barriers to growth – in a deliberate and cyclical form. These OMs tended to modify their own behaviour and the direction of the business in line with the outcome of their reflections. Some OMs engaged in some form of reflection, not in any deliberate way, but rather in an attempt to understand why a particular action appeared to succeed or fail. This unconscious process of reflection appeared to be less focused on an analysis of their own abilities and assumptions, but often resulted in a re-evaluation of their 'world view' and an adjustment in behaviour and direction. Other OMs appeared not to engage in any form of self-reflection and only limited reflection on the performance of the business, appearing to 'meander' through periods of relative success and failure without any attempt to understand the underlying reasons for either. The evidence suggests that owner-managers who engage consciously or unconsciously in reflective practice enlarge their 'competitive footprint' and enhance the performance of their business. The case studies reported below indicate the relationship between the reflective practitioner and the four key factors outlined above.

A total of 16 case studies were produced in the course of the project, from which five have been selected for analysis within the scope of this article. The cases have been selected on the basis of their sectoral relevance and the quality of the data available. The chosen cases show a range of conscious and unconscious reflection. They also demonstrate a range of OM ambitions along a continuum from very little ambition (Case 4) to significant personal and business ambition (Case 5). However it is important to note that *all* reflected the four dimensions of the module. Further research is planned with a larger sample to improve our understanding of the *degrees* of reflection.

Findings

Case study 1: MR1

Introduction

MR1 is a menswear retailer based in the South Wales valleys. This family-owned business was founded over 40 years ago and enjoyed initial success as a well-respected local company. More recently customers opted for brand-named products sold by the large multiple stores and demand for suits, which had been one of their best-selling lines, declined significantly. The opening of a large outlet mall nearby selling leading brands at discount prices could have struck a fatal blow for MR1, but when the current OM took over the business from his father he decided to explore the possibilities that the internet could offer the company. The business is doing well and expanding in a very difficult economic environment.

The ambition of the owner-manager

The OM at MR1 has considerable ambition for himself and the business. The retail business has expanded and become specialist in formalwear hire and clothes for large men. Both ventures have proved successful, creating two new dot.com companies in addition to the original retail operation. He is continually looking for new opportunities to expand the scope of the operation and the turnover.

Location

The business remains in its original premises in the western valley, where overheads are low. The company has recently taken possession of a unit on a local industrial estate from which they run their internet businesses. The OM recognises the advantages of maintaining a low cost base, and now that 60% of turnover comes from national and international internet sales and hire, the location of a retail outlet becomes less significant.

The owner-manager's awareness of the market

The OM at MR1 is very well aware of the market. He is constantly analysing market trends and prices, and monitors retail and on-line competitor activities. Specialising in large sizes was a direct response to market demand. Customers requiring extra-large sizes reported that they are often embarrassed to shop in the on-trend fashion stores, so the internet was an obvious channel through which their needs could be met. The decision to create separate companies to deal with the three key areas of the business allows each to respond to the nuances of their own environment – one size definitely does not fit all – yet they can benefit from shared overheads and scale economies.

Differentiation of product or service offering

MR1 is pursuing a differentiated strategy. This strategy was formulated in response to the changing needs of the market, the impact of a recession and continued economic pressures. Their innovative *modus operandi* allows MR1 to offer customers increased choice at a competitive price. The formalwear hire responds to social change – trends in wedding arrangements, the growth of school and college proms, the increasing popularity of cruise holidays. Through reflective practice the OM has observed and responded to these environmental factors.

Reflective practice

The OM at MR1 consciously engages in reflective practice, though he would not use the term to explain how he evaluates what works and what does not. Not only does he evaluate his own practice and the performance of his own business, he also reflects on other successes and failures within the industry. There is definitive evidence of single-loop learning.

Case study 2: MR2

Introduction

MR2 is a menswear retailer with a base in West Wales, a branch in the suburbs of Cardiff and a branch in the valleys. Since the research was completed, the company have opened a new branch in the south-east area. This is a family business that expanded into South-East Wales by acquiring small menswear retailers that would otherwise have been closed down due to the market conditions outlined in MR1. This expansion demonstrates their continued success despite the prevailing competitive pressures.

The ambition of the owner manager

The OM in MR2 believes that there will be very limited prospects for growth in the traditional retail market and that growth will therefore only be achieved through critical mass and diversification. Expanding the number of outlets and focusing on formalwear hire is MR2s response to their own experiences and the current business environment. So far the strategy is proving successful. The OM considers providing local employment to be an important reason to grow the business.

Location

The OM's experience has shown that when it comes to weddings, proms and celebratory balls, men prefer to hire the appropriate attire. The owner-manager explained that when hiring formalwear customers prefer to stay close to home, having a personal service and convenience for fitting, collecting and returning the garments. Thus, their location, close to the customer, is seen as a positive advantage.

The owner-manager's awareness of the market

The OM at MR2 is very aware of the market in which he operates. He understands the demographic, the social habits and the consumer behaviour of the local communities that make up his customer base. Like MR1, MR2 has recognised the importance of a web presence, but only to advertise the company and its services. They do not trade on line, nor do they wish to reach a wider geographical market, preferring to gain greater market share in a *very* localised market.

Differentiation of product or service offering

The company still considers itself to be a *retailer*, though the formalwear hire represents a significant proportion of the turnover. The company are committed to personal service which they believe the chain stores cannot provide. The OM believes that focussing on formalwear hire will protect the company from the effects of the ongoing recession, as weddings are the last occasion to be sacrificed when budgets are constrained.

Reflective practice

This OM is a reflective practitioner, learning from what has worked in one location and transferring that knowledge to other branches. His approach to reflective practice is perhaps less deliberate than MR1, but there is clear evidence of a learning cycle, the promotion and sharing of good practice and a desire to 'do better'.

Case study 3: WR1

Introduction

WR1 was, at the time the data were gathered, a dress designer with a retail outlet in an affluent suburb of Cardiff. The shop was in a fashionable street of independent retailers, bars and cafes. The OM had been running a successful business offering *haut couture* design in Cardiff for several years. After years of working from home, the OM opened the store to provide a permanent base from which to run her expanding design business. She also made a limited range of 'off the peg' garments to display and sell from the shop, which she hoped would attract new customers to *haut couture*. The design business continues to flourish but the retail outlet was closed within 12 months.

The ambition of the owner-manager

The OM of WR1 is undoubtedly ambitious as a designer of *haut couture* and had already developed a loyal following of customers for her distinctive style. She sees herself as a designer, not a retailer nor an entrepreneur. Her strategy for the shop was to promote her designing service. If the strategy were to succeed she would not *need* to *be* a retailer in the traditional sense. The OM's ambitions were concerned with the creative process rather than the 'selling' process. Within 12 months of opening, she decided to close the store.

Location

The location appeared ideal to capture the target market for WR1. However, the OM had been unable to open the shop during normal retail hours because of her commitments to visiting clients at home, and therefore many opportunities to attract 'passing trade' were lost. It might even have created a negative image of the business. Location is far less important to the design operation and therefore the location did not add confer any significant competitive advantage.

The owner-manager's awareness of the market

The OM had a very well developed understanding of the market for high fashion. The store was decorated to a high standard. Promotional materials, bags and wrappings were also of a high quality. The 'off the peg' range was of very high quality and priced beyond the means of the average shopper, but lacked the cache of an established 'designer' label. Loyal customers continued to opt for bespoke designs. It soon became clear that it would not be possible to satisfy the demands of *haut couture* and up-market retail customers.

Differentiation of product or service offering

The haut couture product was highly differentiated and commanded a premium price. There are relatively few designers of this quality operating in the principality. Unfortunately, the success of this aspect of the business did not prepare the OM for the challenges of retailing. The limited success of the off-the-peg range suggests this 'hybrid' approach falls into what Michael Porter (1980) called 'stuck in the middle' being neither differentiated nor low cost.

Reflective practice

There was very limited evidence of reflective practice informing the decision to open or close the retail business. The OM regarded the experience as a sort of experiment that did not work. The closure of the business allowed the OM to refocus on the design business which had previously proved successful. This is consistent with previous research into SMEs in the creative industries where their reflective practice is reserved for their artistic practice (Ringwald, Harris, & Luo, 2006).

Case study 4: SS1

Introduction

SS1 is a family-owned bakery and sandwich shop with two branches, one in a disadvantaged suburb of Cardiff and one in a more affluent suburb of the city. Each branch has an independent owner-manager. The smaller outlet in the disadvantaged suburb – the subject of this case study – sells high-quality bread and cakes made at the larger branch. Originally this branch was at the heart of a busy community. Located in a small plaza of about six retail outlets, close to a large manufacturing facility, on the edge of a housing estate and close to a school and community college, the business served the people that lived and worked in the area. Unfortunately, the factory has been closed for several years; most of the other shops in the plaza are closed. The housing estate is suffering from the social problems associated with an area of high unemployment and the shop is now dependent on the lunchtime trade from the school and college to support its ever-reducing bread sales. The business faces a very uncertain future and will not survive without a radical change of fortune.

The ambition of the owner-manager

The OM at SS1 is dedicated to the business in which he has spent most of his adult life. He is proud of the high-quality products they have on offer. He hopes that the business will survive, but he cannot see how the company can compete with the low prices and choice offered by the supermarkets. His ambition is to see the business continue into the next generation.

Location

The location, once an asset, is now a distinct disadvantage. What market remains locally is price-sensitive and unwilling or unable to pay a premium price for high-quality goods. However, it appears that no consideration has been given to relocating to another part of the city and they have no plans to open new branches in developing areas, e.g. the popular waterfront area with extensive housing developments, bars, cafes and restaurants, which would be just the area for high-quality, locally produced bread and cakes. No consideration had been given to a mobile sandwich business.

The owner-manager's awareness of the market

The OM at SS1 was well aware of the market conditions in the immediate vicinity of the shop. There seemed to be very limited communication between the two branches and therefore limited opportunities for exchange of ideas, etc. Though well aware of the threats from supermarkets, the OM seemed less aware of the growing demand for locally produced food and the opportunity that might present. Against his personal preference, the OM had recently introduced more 'junk food' to appeal to the school children.

Differentiation of product or service delivery

There has been no recent innovation in product or service delivery. The OM's energies are focused on maintaining turnover, managing security issues and trying to balance supply and demand to minimise waste. The OM firmly believes that the quality of the product is the company's greatest asset.

Reflective practice

This is a SIR at a critical point in its lifecycle. Though the OM reflects on its current plight, he does not reflect on his own practice, nor does he consider how organisational knowledge and learning could inform decisions regarding the company's future. Access to a mentor who may be able to encourage the OM to consider his situation through a process of critical reflection would certainly be of benefit in this case.

Case study 5: HD1

Introduction

HD1 is a unisex hairdresser and beautician which also sells personal grooming products for men and women. The shop, in an attractive city centre location, is one of five owned and operated by a family with an international reputation as hair-dressing champions. In this branch the OM is a young woman who has grown up in the business. This salon is very successful and considered a model of good practice within the family.

Ambition of the owner-manager

The OM is ambitious for the business, not in terms of profitability, but to be the *best* establishment in the city, and expects her staff to share this ambition. She believes that customers will respond to 'the best' by recommending the salon to friends and family. It already has a very loyal client base.

Location

The city centre location places HD1 in close proximity to other high-quality salons. The family already has salons in the affluent suburbs. This salon attracts customers who work in the city or who will travel to the city centre to access quality products and services. The OM sees this as the 'flagship' salon, with a high profile.

The owner-manager's awareness of the market

The OM has a very well developed understanding of the market – not surprising, given her family's involvement over many years. She is aware of local competition and national trends in the business. Brand is becoming increasingly important. Fashion conscious customers want to be associated with prestigious salons and even individual stylists. The recent emergence of multiples like Toni & Guy have impacted on the industry, but the OM feels that the strength of their brand can compete in the local market. They started to sell the grooming products in response to customer demand and they sell high-quality products at commensurate prices.

Differentiation of product and service delivery

The OM considers this to be their great strength. They strive to be 'the best' in quality and service. They provide a very personal touch. The staff are trained to give advice and guidance to customers. They build on personal relationships. They want only the best staff and their staff turnover is low.

Reflective practice

The OM in HD1 is a conscious reflective practitioner. She is constantly reviewing what works and what does not. She includes her staff in the process and she also learns from other salons in the family chain, though not all are as ambitious or successful as HD1. Her infectious enthusiasm is central to the 'vibe' within the business. She has considerable personal ambition and she regularly reflects on her own performance, beliefs and assumption in order to remain 'in touch' with the business.

Discussion

The case studies illustrate the competitive 'footprint' of each SIR. MR1 and HD1 have the largest 'footprint', demonstrating strength in each of the four key factors. The OMs are ambitious for their organisations and exhibit creative and inclusive leadership styles. The importance of leadership in retail development has previously been recognised by Duckett and Macfarlane (2002). Their locations are thoughtfully and effectively chosen to fit with the long-term objectives of the organisation. Previous research suggests that a strategic approach to location decision-making is rare in SMEs generally and retail businesses in particular (Pioch & Byrom, 2004). Both businesses have found a product and service 'mix' that suits their customer base. This 'mix' has been achieved through a customer-centred approach and a shift, as Knee (2002, p. 526) describes, from a 'push' system of 'sell what you buy' to a 'pull' system of 'buy what you sell'. The most significant advantage MR1 and HD1 have is an understanding of their respective markets. This is supported by the work of Lee, Johnson and Gahring (2008) which advocates continual scanning of markets and the dynamics of those markets. Both have successfully identified and exploited market segments by crafting appropriate marketing strategies. These advantages have been achieved through the direction of OMs who recognise the need for reflection-in-action and reflection-on-action (Schon, 1983), consciously using reflective practice to analyse, evaluate and shape their operations.

MR2 shares many of the advantages of MR1, though the OM takes a less formal approach to reflective practice. Their locations are strategically well chosen and their product and service offerings have been developed to meet local market need. The OM is less ambitious for the business than MR1, seeing the current development and expansion as a necessary means to withstand the pressures from the 'big box' competitors – representing a defensive position rather than an expansionary one. Both MR1 and MR2 reflect on their 'obligation' to provide a service to the local community. For MR1 this means providing local employment and maintaining a physical presence in their home town. For MR2 it is also about providing a community service through its integration in the local economy and by developing a strong identity with the place and the people (Coca-Stefaniak et al., 2010). Pioch and Byrom (2004) suggest that this sensitivity about the community may be stronger in Wales than elsewhere in the UK. This will be considered in future research.

WR1 is an interesting example of an artist/designer being reflective in her creative practice, but quite the opposite in her approach to retailing. This is consistent with previous research (Ringwald, et al., 2006), which suggests that entrepreneurs in the creative industries are artists first and entrepreneurs second, and while they are able to critically reflect on their *artistic* practice, they do not engage in the same way with *business* practice.

SS1 showed little evidence of reflective practice. The OM reflected on the general economic environment, but did not reflect in any meaningful way on how his business might respond to the ever-increasing environmental pressures. This case does not demonstrate an *unwillingness* to change but a total lack of understanding as to *what might usefully be changed* in any of the four key factors.

These cases are representative of the larger sample produced during 2009 and 2010, which suggest that in order to increase the 'competitive footprint' SIRs need to engage in and respond to critical reflection. The study indicates that, if OMs engage in reflective practice, they *can* identify opportunities to enhance performance in the four key aspects of the business.

The role of reflective practice

Reflective practice appears to provide the link between the four factors in the model and how those factors contribute to the success of the business. All of the OMs acknowledged that the four factors are significant, but only the reflective practitioners appear to enhance organisational performance along each dimension. For example, all of the OMs interviewed recognised the importance of location, but only a few used locational factors to their advantage.

Jack and Anderson (1999) define reflective practitioners as 'individuals who, through their knowledge and critical ability, are capable not only of starting new businesses but also ensuring the continuing viability of the businesses by enhancing the capacity for them to develop through a richer understanding of the entrepreneurial process' (p. 111). They refer to the entrepreneurial process as 'the extraction of value from the environment ... usually in a novel way' (p. 113) – an environment which they describe as uncertain and idiosyncratic in nature. The role of reflective practice for SIRs would therefore appear to be to enhance *entrepreneurial practice*, with our four-factor model being the bridge that links retail operations with entrepreneurial skill.

Given that many OMs will have many pressures on their time (Pioch & Byrom, 2004), any model of reflective practice needs to be easy to understand and simple to execute. The process of critical reflection can be both lonely and emotional (Chivers, 2003), which may cause some OMs to disengage with the process. Chivers (2003) and Broadridge (1999) suggest that mentoring OMs through the process of critical reflection might concentrate the entrepreneurial mind and give the OM confidence to act on the basis of the reflective process.

Summary and conclusions

This article has given some insights into the factors affecting the survival of SIRs, in particular the ambitions of the OMs, locational decisions, the understanding of the market and the environment and the relevance of the product and service offering. It has also identified and explored the extent to which reflective practice determines the *competitive footprint*.

The evidence from this study suggests that there is indeed a link between reflective practice and the survival of SIRs, which warrants further research. There are four key areas which we propose to explore:

(1) The development of a self-assessment instrument which will enable SIRs to measure their competitive footprint. The instrument to be based on measuring the extent of their critical reflection on each of the four factors.

(2) The value of mentoring to the OM (in terms of support) through the process of reflective practice and the impact of mentoring on the quality of process outcomes.

(3) The significance of the sector or context in which the business operates on the relative importance of each of the four factors.

(4) In the longer term, to test the general applicability of the findings by extending the study beyond the borders of Wales.

Given the increasing interest in urban regeneration, rural sustainability and the 'big society', the future research could inform local and central governments' policy regarding support for SMEs wherein SIRs have hitherto been sadly neglected.

References

Bennison, D., Clarke, I., & Pal, J. (2005). Locational decision making in retailing: An exploratory framework for analysis. *The International Review of Retail, Distribution and Consumer Research*, *5*(1), 1–20.

Bennison, D., Warnaby, G., & Pal, J. (2010). Local shopping in the UK: Towards a synthesis of business and place. *International Journal of Retail Management & Distribution Management*, *38*(11), 846–864.

Broadridge, A. (1999). Mentoring in retailing: A tool for success? *Personnel Review*, *28*(4), 336–355.

Chivers, G. (2003). Utilising reflective practice interviews in professional development. *Journal of European Industrial Training*, *27*, 5–15.

Coca-Stefaniak, J.A., Parker, C., & Rees, P. (2010). Localisation as a marketing strategy for small retailers. *International Journal of Retail & Distribution Management*, *38*(9), 677–697.

Dawson, J.A. (1983). Independent retailing in Great Britain: Dinosaur or chameleon? *Retail & Distribution Management*, *May/June*, 29–32.

Duckett, H., & Macfarlane, E. (2002). Emotional intelligence and transformational leadership in retailing. *Leadership and Organization Development Journal*, *24*, 309–317.

Elms, J., Canning, C., de Kervenoael, R., Whysall, P., & Hallsworth, A. (2010). Thirty years of retail change: Where (and how) do you shop? *International Journal of Retail & Distribution Management*, *38*(10/12), 807–820.

Guy, C. (2010). Revival of the fittest. *Town and Coutry Planning, January*, 11–13.

House of Commons All-Party Parliamentary Small Shops Group. (2006). *High Street Britain 2015*.

Jack, S.L., & Anderson, A.R. (1999). Entrepreneurship education within the enterprise culture. Producing reflective practitioners. *International Journal of Entrepreneurial Behaviour & Research*, *5*(3), 110–125.

Knee, C. (2002). Learning from experience: Five challenges for retailers. *International Journal of Retail and Distribution Management*, *30*(11), 518–529.

Lee, S.E., Johnson, K.K.P., & Gahring, S.A. (2008). Small-town consumers' disconfirmation of expectations and satisfaction with local independent suppliers. *International Journal of Retail and Distribution Management*, *36*(2), 143–157.

National Retail Planning Forum (NRPF). (2004). *The role and vitality of secondary shopping – a new direction*. London: National Retail Planning Forum.

Pioch, E., & Byram, J. (2004). Small independent retail firms and locational decision-making: Outdoor leisure retailing by the crags. *Journal of Small Business & Enterprise Development*, *11*(2), 222–232.

Porter, M.E. (1980). *Competitive strategy*. New York: Free Press.

Ringwald, K., Harris, J., & Luo, L. (2006). *The Doctor Who effect: The emergence of a creative industries cluster in South East Wales.* Paper presented at the ISBE Conference, Cardiff, November 2006.

Schon, D.A. (1983). *The reflective practitioner: How professionals think in action.* London: Maurice Temple Smith.

A longitudinal reflection of blended/reflexive enterprise and entrepreneurial education

Jonathan Deacon and Jacqueline Harris

University of Wales, Newport, UK

This article seeks to investigate the experiences, aspirations and outcomes of participants on the MA Business and Enterprise Development (MA BED) programme at the Newport Business School as interpreted through their own reflective practice. The development of an enterprise programme within the Newport Business School arose from the need to provide relevant enterprise-related education and support to students seeking to develop their enterprise skills and entrepreneurial aspirations; it also complemented government policy at the time. The investigation takes a longitudinal approach and further seeks to explore the pedagogic success (or not) of a blended enterprise education and entrepreneurship education masters programme from the participants' standpoint. Results suggest that a blended/reflective pedagogic approach to enterprise and entrepreneurship education has value in developing a wider range of skills within participants and also has a greater effect on aspiration. In this case 'aspiration' appears to be closely linked to an individual's confidence (a likelihood that they will be positively predisposed to negative circumstances) which in turn has a disproportionate (positive) effect on their ability to identify and rationalise opportunity. The latter reference to rationalisation appears linked to the higher-level thinking (reflective practice: both reflection and reflexivity) and analytical skills developed throughout the masters programme.

Introduction

The MA Business and Enterprise Development (MA BED) programme was a post-graduate qualification with three stages: a certificate; diploma; and masters stage (one-year full-time/two-year part-time). The objectives of the programme were to provide within the University of Wales, Newport: 'support to encourage and develop entrepreneurship'. The structure and content of the programme was developed around three key themes:

(1) the person;
(2) the environment; and
(3) the business opportunity.

The qualification addressed the need to provide relevant higher education to support the innovation, creative and entrepreneurial development of individuals within new and existing small firms. The programme aimed to provide students with an understanding of entrepreneurial and intrapreneurial business activities, to enable them to enhance and develop their own or others' required knowledge, skills and attitude in starting up, running or developing further a small business or enterprise. Teaching and learning within the programme was a blended approach of lectures, workshops, guest speakers/lecturers and Q&A (war stories) sessions with business people/entrepreneurs and policymakers. Students had the opportunity to participate in and attend networking and business support sessions in partnership with the Welsh Assembly Government and the local Regional Development Agency (RDA) (Newport and Gwent Enterprise). The method of assessment throughout the programme was 'reflexive', an approach to behavioural change (Osterman & Kottkamp, 2004) that had been successfully used to develop entrepreneurial behaviour and practice before (see Jones-Evans, Williams, & Deacon, 2000). Thus, the blending of a multitude of externalised pedagogic stimuli with a personalised reflective element was planned to answer the critique of 'management education' of Cunningham (1991) when he observed that professional business performance (and thus entrepreneurial behaviour) is a function of the successful combination of knowledge, skills and attitude; then typically education at masters level has focused on the first of these, largely ignored the second and assumed that the third is inherent within the student. Whilst one can argue that much has changed since Cunningham wrote his critique (and indeed that much has not), one thing that appears to have been largely overlooked in the entrepreneurship literature is the concept of 'refection-in-action' and the use of reflective practice to enhance entrepreneurial attitude. The BED teaching team consisted of academic staff but mainly practitioners (in a ratio of about 2:1), some of whom had been or were still involved in setting up and running businesses or were specialists in areas such as marketing, finance, business support and venture capital funding.

The programme targeted the development of skills that would:

- enable and encourage the support and creation of new business(es);
- be used in existing small and medium enterprises (SMEs), by those working in the area of business support;
- allow individuals looking to achieve a personal goal through starting and developing their own business idea or enterprise opportunity;
- enable those in larger organisations where the need for innovative intrapreneurial skills would become increasingly important to the future economy; and
- develop lifelong 'reflexive' skills.

The programme was accredited as a University of Wales qualification, and the Welsh European Funding Office confirmed approval in June 2002 for an initial two-year project. The MA BED programme continued for a total of five years (five cohorts). In the final three years, students were recruited on a self-funding basis (no European Social Fund (ESF) bursary support available). After the initial two-year ESF project period, the programme was placed in the school's mainstream course portfolio and was removed from the portfolio in 2007 and enterprise education was introduced as a (non-reflexive) 'theme' in a restructured MBA.

Background literature

Historic context of enterprise education

Small has become beautiful once again – especially from an economic development point of view. This attractiveness stems from the recognition that small firm birth, development and growth has an acknowledged centrality as a necessary competitive instrument to a 'modern, vibrant and progressive economy' (Beaver & Prince, 2004, p. 34); further, the importance of the sector to the growth and well-being of an economy is underlined by the interest shown by researchers from: business; marketing; socio-economics; politics; and social regeneration (Beaver & Carr, 2002; Stanworth & Gray, 1991).

During the 1980s, a new foundation to the economy emerged primarily in the US and primarily based within the computer industry. It was an economic evolution that had as its driver a dynamic business sector made up of small firms that were managed in very entrepreneurial and informal ways – especially in the software and biotechnology sectors (Thurik & Wennekers, 2004). The work of Birch (1979) became central to the policy thrust in the American economy for the establishment, development and growth of the small and entrepreneurial firm (Timmons, 1999; Gibb & Davis, 1990), while in the UK the early 1980s saw spiralling unemployment and political unrest (Storey & Johnson, 1987). Indeed, Thurik and Wennekers (2004, p. 143) comment: 'as Europe's unemployment soared into double digits and growth stagnated, the capacity of the US entrepreneurial economy to generate both jobs and higher wages became the object of envy'.

However, it is argued (Jones & Iredale, 2010) that the basis for change had already begun within UK education for a more 'enterprise' focussed curricular to better fit the requirements of business and industry (or certainly the future needs). Jones and Iredale highlight the 'Ruskin' speech given by James Callaghan at Ruskin College, Oxford in 1976, as the birthplace for many contemporary views on enterprise education, as Callaghan identified that there was a skills shortfall at the time, (alluding to enterprise skills) and that education and industry needed to foster closer links in order to develop more appropriate curricular to develop the economy, and thereby improve society through wealth creation (Callaghan, 1976). The speech became a catalyst for progressive education reforms, resulting in the development of a National Curriculum and the introduction of Technical and Vocational Education Initiative (TVEI), the latter aimed at developing 'non-curricular' skills especially in students who were not motivated by 'normative' academic attainment. The TVEI initiative was seen as part of a 'new vocationalism' within education and can be identified as 'laying the foundation for enterprise education' (Jones & Iredale, 2010, p. 9).

An (evolutionary) economy context

Evolutionary economists and social scientists (for example, see Penrose, 1959; Kauffman, 1993; Romer, 1994) will argue that to stimulate an entrepreneurial economy (one that has the right mix of firms at the various stages of growth and maturity to sustain economic well-being) a cultural (and implicit educational) shift needs to take place and not simply a change of political policy (Entrepreneurial Action Plan for Wales [EAP], 1999). Indeed, the view that national and regional economies are successful *because* of evolutionary shifts is supported by many who share the

Schumpeter (1934) 'creative destruction' stance (European Union., 2003), and the consequential and obvious outcome of such policy: that there is a need to encourage and develop a constant stream of 'new' entrepreneurs who are opportunistic of, and adaptive to, dynamic business environments (Giunipero, Denslow, & Eltantawy, 2005).

Bjerke and Hultman (2002) suggest that there are many signs to indicate that small firms will be most able to capitalise on opportunities emerging from the dynamic socio-economic situations. The ability for small firms to adapt to evolving social change and seize opportunities through innovation can be seen as a necessity for survival. However, by necessity, this calls for the owner/manager/entrepreneur/ employee to be equipped with the skills to adapt to the economic dynamic. The debate surrounding the development of entrepreneurial skills (nature/nurture) continues (see, for example, Henry, Hill, & Leitch, 2005); however, a growing body of academic research suggests that entrepreneurship can be taught (Kuratko, 2005); and further, those entrepreneurs that have had exposure to higher education are more likely to have a global view, be faster to adapt existing business models and integrate technology earlier in the business development phase (Scase, 2007). Given this level of sophistication, these entrepreneurs are therefore thought more likely to use high-level skills in developing ventures and therefore add greater value to regional economies (Minniti & Levesque, 2008).

In a UK context the Department of Trade and Industry (DTI), through the 'Enterprise in Higher Education Initiative' (Whiteley, 1995), pursued education policies that developed an understanding of the skills needed for both employed work and self-employed work, and encouraged closer links between business and education and, in particular, business leaders and educationalists, thus developing a future workforce that is 'enterprising' within different contexts (Department of Trade and Industry [DTI], 2000, 2001). This 'entrepreneurial mindset' is thought central to enable societies and the firms within them to cope with the ambiguity and complexity of contemporary economic structures. However, as Taatila (2010, p. 49) critically observes: 'unfortunately, the current situation of support for entrepreneurship in higher education lacks depth, at least within the EU. Only about 24% of university students have access to any education on entrepreneurship. The more focussed the subject branch the less likelihood there is of a student learning entrepreneurial skills'.

Definitional ambiguity

There is without doubt great ambiguity with both the definition of the term 'enterprise education' and the context in which the term is increasingly used, as Jones and Iredale (2010) comment: 'enterprise education is a chimera that can mean all things to all people – enterprise and entrepreneurship education are perceived to be conflated terms that for many in the education and business communities mean much the same thing'. The definitional issue appears to stem from the apparent frequent substitution of the terms enterprise and entrepreneurship within an educational context and often by policymakers and within academic debate. Such definitional misappropriation is not uncommon within the business and management discipline, as linguistic use produces meaning through narrative in context (Deacon, 2008).

However, Gibb (1993) suggests that enterprise education has a focus upon the development of skills, behaviours and attributes which can inform an individual's future approach to problem-solving, so in essence a 'mindset'. Gibb (1993) continues and differentiates enterprise education from 'entrepreneurship education', suggesting that the latter is more clearly about business start up and development. Jones and Iredale (2010) discuss the definitional problem at length in their paper and conclude: 'entrepreneurship education focuses primarily on the needs of the entrepreneur, whereas enterprise education addresses the requirements of a wider range of stakeholders, including consumers and the wider community' (2010, p. 11). Whereas Jones and English (2004, p. 416) define entrepreneurial education as 'a process of providing individuals with the ability to recognise commercial opportunities and the insight, self-esteem, knowledge and skills to act on them'. Nevertheless, Jamison's typology of entrepreneurial education is of value to this article. Jamieson (1984) proposed three distinct classes of entrepreneurial education:

(1) About enterprise;
(2) For enterprise; and
(3) In enterprise.

The MA BED programme focussed firmly on the latter two of these classes (but did consider the first), concurring with the views of Herrmann, Hannon, Cox, Ternouth, and Crowley (2008) when they posit that entrepreneurial education should be less transitional (learning 'about') and more experiential (learning 'for'). Thus, the MA BED programme structure allowed for a general understanding about entrepreneurship as a phenomenon within society (Hytti & O'Gorman, 2004), moved to a focus on the creation of a venture (Co & Mitchell, 2006) and considered in detail the development of innovative and creative management thinking for those within existing organisations (corporate enterprising) (Kirby, 2004).

Entrepreneurial pedagogy or experiential andragogy

The development of pedagogy within enterprise and entrepreneurial education is well documented within extant literature (Pittway & Cope, 2007). The central feature of much of the literature surrounding 'entrepreneurial education' is the development of a blended pedagogic and experiential learning intervention (see, for example, Cunningham, 1991; Jack & Anderson, 1999; Jones-Evans et al., 2000; Matlay, 2006; Jones & Iredale, 2006; Volkmann et al., 2009), Jones and Iredale (2010, p. 12) making the distinction that enterprise education is and can be developed across subject areas, whereas entrepreneurship education is typically delivered in higher education (HE) via business school modules.

In either case, the role of the 'lecturer' is key, as she or he adopt facilitation and mentoring approaches to individual reflexive development as opposed to 'normative' didactic approaches. Jones and Iredale (2010) comment on this advance: 'the challenge for the lecturer is to develop a teaching style that encourages learning by doing, exchange, experiment, positive mistake-making, calculated risk-taking, creative problem-solving and interaction with the outside world' (p. 12); they conclude: 'students also need to learn to adapt to this distinctive approach to teaching and learning, which requires interaction and independent thought' (p. 12). Further, commenting on the contemporary entrepreneurial skills of European HE academics, Taatila (2010, p. 49) observes: 'the competence and time allocated by academic staff to entrepreneurial education is inadequate', especially in reference to the aspiration of governments that see entrepreneurs and entrepreneurial ventures driving regional and national economies out of recession.

Controversially, how and when learning/development takes place is less easy to define and measure in entrepreneurial students, perhaps due in part to the holistic nature of skill attainment within entrepreneurship education, the inverse of the 'atomised' approach used in 'traditional' theory based teaching (Rae, 2000). Therefore 'pragmatic' learning environments are key to the development of entrepreneurial competence (where psychological and social skills are enhanced) where a 'real world' complexity is acknowledged and 'factual' certainties are rare (Bennis & O'Toole, 2005), 'pragmatism is focussed on education for or in enterprise, acquiring knowledge in real-life situations is neither inductive nor deductive, but an abductive process ... where learning should be inner-directed' (Taatila, 2010, p. 56), and where reflexive practices have great educational value. To some extent such a debate is incomplete without reference to the literature on 'strengths-based education' (Holland, 1994); however, such strengths-based approaches in organizational settings have empathy within entrepreneurial education in that the teaching/learning methodology shifts from the participants knowledge weaknesses (knowledge deficits) to the strengths (knowledge assets).

In his conclusion, Taatila poses several questions for those who are involved in developing entrepreneurial education; these focus on the tension between the 'normative' theory-based approach taken to teaching and learning by universities and the 'pragmatic' contextual, experiential and reflexive approach needed to develop entrepreneurial graduates, the most pertinent is illustrated thus:

> should there be some type of motivational course for all students in higher education institutions in order to present the positive sides of entrepreneurship? The present environment, at least from a Finnish perspective, tends to stress the risks related to a self-managed career. (Taatila, 2010, p. 57)

However, empirical based studies based in organisational settings like that of Taatila are rare in contemporary literature, as are studies that seek insight into the development of reflexive practice-based entrepreneurial education.

Summation

Thus, entrepreneur and entrepreneurial educationalists find themselves in a postmodern educational paradox, where they face a paradoxical juxtaposition of oppositional views in that, at a corporate level, many HE institutions espouse the concept of enterprise as it relates to a university setting, yet within the academic school setting the risks of achieving a 'self actualised' state in the form of self-employment or employer (self-managed career) is stressed and reinforced through pedagogic assessment and administrative structures. If the educationalist is therefore to adopt an asset-based approach and create customised curricular within specialised learning environments, that have positive and longitudinal impact (VanTassel-Baska, 1994), it is highly likely that they, too, are entrepreneurial and enterprising and work within the gaps that are created by academic administrative structures. Thus, this (ongoing) study offers insight into the development of a reflexive-based educational programme and how such intervention has impacted upon the participants over time – aspects which are not fully developed in extant literature.

Methodology

In order to investigate the outcomes of the MA BED programme – especially with a focus on: the longitudinal impact of the programme on participants experiences, aspirations and reflections; and the use of a blended/reflective approach to enterprise education and entrepreneurship education (thus a programme 'about', 'for' and 'in' entrepreneurship) – we take a mixed method approach and employ quantitative and qualitative methods of data generation and data analysis.

The design had two distinct phases of enquiry and analysis – where the qualitative analysis will supplement the initial quantitative data.

Phase One

Instruments used in phase one of the study therefore have initially been based on a factual quantitative analysis and reporting of data generated by course documentation (the reflective journals of the students) and student records. The reflective journals were analysed through a process of recursive abstraction (Stebbins, 2001) which developed 'base' themes without the need for detailed coding that were then used as the departure points for the second phase of the study.

Phase Two

Phase two was developed by in-depth open-ended reflexive (responsive) interviewing of a sample (self-selection) of the participants, where an interpretivist approach to data analysis through an iterative process (Weik, 1995; Holliday, 2007) developed phase one themes that have subsequently been further explored using the same analytical method within phase three of the ongoing study.

The use of an iterative approach is a recommended method for researching socially constructed phenomena and has its precedent in Deacon (2008). Carson, Gilmore, and Grant (2001, p. 7) suggest that the interpretivist approach allows the research to gain an insight to the social construction of meaning in relation to a given context, 'the aim is to understand and explain why people (actors) have different experiences, rather than search for external causes and fundamental laws to explain their behaviour'.

The units of analysis in the study are drawn from the 68 students that enrolled on the programme and participated in one or more stages of the programme. Samples were self-selecting after an initial email or hard copy communication from the researchers, as at this stage the study design did not want to pre-determine the input or output characteristics of the participants, but instead just wanted the data to evolve in order to gain insight and richness.

Results and discussion: phase one – quantitative data

Recruitment

The total number of students recruited to the programme over the five years was 68 (see Table 1). Of this number, 40 students were recruited over the two years that the programme was funded through European Social Funding and where students had access, if eligible, to bursary monies to pay for fees, equipment and travel. During this period the programme also recruited five students that were self-funded (non-ESF support).

Table 1. Number of students recruited to programme.

ESF funded	
Cohort 1	13
Cohort 2	27*
Total	40
Non-ESF funded	
Cohort 3[†]	15
Cohort 4[†]	6
Cohort 5	7
Total	28
Recruitment total (all years)	68

Notes: [†]denotes international student(s) recruited: cohort 3 = 4; cohort 4 = 1.*Includes five self-funded students (i.e. not eligible for ESF bursary support).

The most successful year for recruitment was year two of the programme. This would suggest that ESF support has, during this time, a positive effect on student recruitment, as subsequent years' recruitment figures, although acceptable initially, waned. The non-ESF-supported years recruited, in total, only 28 students.

Retention

In terms of retention, the figures in Table 2 provide some interesting insight. Overall, only 10 students left the programme without completing any part of the taught programme. However, of those that did withdraw, nine were part of the ESF-supported element of the programme (the project) and only one student from the remaining three years of the programme withdrew early. This would suggest that support, in terms of public monies, is no guarantee of a student's completion/achievement on a course of education, be it entrepreneurial or not, and that for self-funded participants a personal predisposition for completion/achievement was a greater motivation (a behavioural outcome that is concurrent with the entrepreneurial attitude of self-efficacy). However, it could be hypothesised that, the programme gained intrinsic value in the eyes of applicants initially by being supported by public funding, and that early withdrawal from the programme was driven by students

Table 2. Number of students recruited, less early leavers.

	Recruited	Sub total	Early leavers	Totals
Cohort 1	13		2	
Cohort 2	27*	40	7	31
Cohort 3	15			
Cohort 4	6		1	
Cohort 5	7	28		27
Total			68	58

Note: *Includes five self-funded students (i.e. not eligible for ESF bursary support).

not being fully aware of content, intention of the programme and perceived suitability to meet aspirations.

Likewise, the tutor team experientially gain insight regarding the type of student suitable for the programme and those who are more likely to complete and/or achieve. Staff with experience of the programme might counsel prospective students accordingly; this could be a reason for the high numbers of withdrawals at the early stage of the programme (staff experience low), and low numbers in later years (staff experience high).

Analysis of the 'reflective journals' shows that for the most part the initial motivation for undertaking the programme was to attain the skills and knowledge required to set up and start a business/develop a business further. For many students, by the diploma stage, they had gained these skills and knowledge and therefore their aspirations had been met; they then exited the programme. Therefore it was only a small minority of students that wished to achieved the 'masters' stage of the programme.

Results: phase two – in-depth reflexive interviews and indications of evolving themes

In 2010 the study moved to the second phase of the research with eight of the programme alumni. A series of in-depth reflexive interviews were carried out that have given indication of emergent themes within the generated data; a longer list of emergent themes were initially proposed (in line with the recursive abstractive approach), but synergies between sub-themes has allowed for subsumation into those which are outlined and briefly discussed below.

Confidence

Initial results suggest that a blended pedagogic approach to enterprise and entrepreneurship education has value in developing a wider range of skills within participants and also has a greater effect on aspiration. In this case 'aspiration' appears to be closely linked to an individual's confidence (a likelihood that they will be positively predisposed to negative circumstances), which in turn has a disproportionate (positive) effect on their ability to identify and rationalise opportunity. The latter reference to rationalisation appears linked to the higher-level thinking (reflective practice: both reflection and reflexivity) and analytical skills developed throughout the masters programme.

Opportunity recognition

The propensity and ability to recognise opportunities appears to be closely linked to the individual's confidence (see above). The ability to assess (rationalise) and act upon (or not) opportunities in light of their experience, capabilities and resource availability was prevalent throughout discussions.

Acceptance of change

Individuals acknowledged their awareness of technology and its part in creating and developing new and fast-moving markets and opportunities and its impact on the pace of change and development of new innovative business models. The events of the past two years (recession) were also acknowledged as one of turbulence and uncertainty. However, despite this commonly perceived 'difficult period', individuals intimated that this did not stop their assessment of, nor would it prevent them from taking action on, an opportunity; though perhaps with more caution than normal (evidence of reflexive behaviours), given the instability of not just local but global economies.

Awareness of commercial environment

Individuals discussed their awareness, and the importance of, developing a sustainable brand and business model. This was discussed in relation to individuals' experience, since completing the programme, of opportunities that they had considered and/or acted upon, in addition to their observations of other business un/successful ventures.

Communicate and use appropriate language

A reflection of the skills and understanding gained during their participation in the programme and an aspect that was considered of high importance was the individual's ability to be able to discuss (using appropriate language) key terms and terminology with professional business service firms (especially those associated with business start up and development), such as accountants and solicitors.

Problem-solving and ambiguity

Discussed in relation to confidence and opportunity recognition, individuals expressed their capacity for approaching and solving problems in a more positive (and creative) way, and their capacity to cope and deal with stress situations that they may previously have perceived as ambiguous in a more creative and constructive manner.

Action and lifelong learning

Individuals acknowledged that their experiences on the programme had provided them with a clearer insight into the benefits of becoming action-learning-oriented (with reflection) and actively sought out new experiences, new opportunities to learn (formal and informal), some of which had impacted on personal as well as professional life pathways.

Conclusions: phase one and two

Thus, this study has indicated uniqueness in two distinct ways. Firstly, the longitudinal 'topic' approach of the methodology as suggested by Carson et al. (2001, p. 219), where accumulated knowledge, insights and understanding can contribute to experiential knowledge development of how the participants have used praxis within their ongoing personal development (thus, the aim of developing lifelong reflexive skills). The study also highlights a paucity of similar 'over time' studies within the extant literature of entrepreneurship and enterprise interventions within a

UK context. And secondly, that the study considers the nature and typology of a 'blended' approach to asset-based learning, blended in this case being the mix of entrepreneurial stimuli interventions from a wide range of sources – including the participants own case histories. Thus, the MA BED was neither a programme 'about' enterprise nor was it 'for' entrepreneurship, but was driven by the participants' self-acknowledged strengths through a series of 'blended' and 'reflexive' steps from recognition (about), through cognition (for), to application (in) and therefore from enterprise education to entrepreneurship education to self actualisation.

The results of the study show clearly that it was attractive to three distinct 'groups' of participants:

(1) Those who found themselves in a role that demanded a greater understanding of 'enterprise' and 'entrepreneurship' (therefore seeking knowledge 'about');
(2) Those who were or had been nascent entrepreneurs and needed 'entrepreneurship education' 'for' venture start up; and
(3) Those who were engaged in a venture and were therefore 'in' enterprise and were seeking enterprise development skills in order to develop the extant venture.

As somewhat predicted, there have been observable outcome and completion differences between those participants who received government bursaries (ESF) and those who were self-funding; however not all nor either fall within the same group dynamic as outlined above.

Implications for practice

An implication of the study suggests that the 'blended/reflective' approach used within the BED programme may have resulted in synergistic benefits to the participants and the 'tutor' team. The extant literature briefly discusses the need for a different approach to delivery of such programmes, and that 'blended' in this educational context refers to the mix of methods used in 'creating' what VanTassel-Baska (1994) refers to as 'specialist learning environments' where the curricular is customized by the participant 'through' socialized participation and reflexivity supported by tutors to further enhance their 'knowledge asset'. An integral part of the 'blended/reflexive' approach was a welcomed (by the participants) move away from reductionist-type delivery as found in other MA/MBA courses. The MA BED, in the need to move along a continuum from recognition through cognition to application, used a holistic and contextual approach to knowledge development. Thus, 'specialist' tutors (finance, marketing, human resources, law) were sought by participants as and when the individual need arose within the course of the programme – and thus an androgenic design.

The MA BED interventions typically took place in the university boardroom and were discursive and free flowing; however, alternative 'non-traditional' venues were also used (at the request of the participants) and included restaurants and pubs, as well as 'site' visits to businesses and policymakers who were part of the 'tutor' team. Such an informal approach sits within the paradox faced by educators within the field of enterprise education, as discussed earlier, and can be dismissed by 'normative' practitioners as a frivolous and neo-liberal approach to education which has little to do with the 'serious' business of business. It is a view that can be 'perhaps' justified by the current lack of conceptual and empirical studies to date – but this study begins to indicate that such approaches to knowledge development can benefit from both a review of historical precedents and the methodologies used in other fields in order to bring clarity and insight into the development of 'blended/reflexive' entrepreneurship programmes. It is also suggested that practitioners of entrepreneurship education curricular may want to develop the 'blended' approach in context for their practice, as this study is beginning to show that it has clear benefits in developing the specialist learning environment needed to develop lifelong entrepreneurial skill sets.

Implications for policy

Taatila (2010) observes that the university system (in his case Finland, but this study suggests more widespread risk-averse institutional culture) promotes and reinforces the negative aspects of entrepreneurship and thus the perceived 'dangers' of the 'self-managed career'. This study has identified that participants are open to and welcome the androgogic approach to development and career, and the study observes that an individual drawn to such a programme is likely to have a pre-disposition to self-direction and thus reflective practice. However, the implication for policy is somewhat wider than that which concentrates on entrepreneurship education. The wider question that arises is one that asks: is there an implicit negative ethos in the fabric of many, if not all, of the content of courses within a university (or scholastic) environment towards self-actualisation? This question gives rise to a second: does such an implicit negativity towards 'self-actualisation' impact on the ability for entrepreneurship scholars to develop and establish specialist curricular? The answer to these questions could have major implications for the development of the economy and therefore wider society in the longer term, but also may shed light on the clear enterprise motivational differentials between countries, as illustrated by the gap between the number of patents applied for and registered in the US and the UK. A 'blended' approach may thus suggest that the use of a wider range of entrepreneurial stimuli – especially stimuli that are delivered by 'non-educationalists' may just go some way to redressing the institutionalised risk-averse culture not just within universities but, perhaps more importantly, within lecture rooms. The ongoing nature of this study, it is hoped, will develop this insight yet further.

Notes

The data presented is analysed by cohort. It does not indicate (at this stage), gender, age, prior knowledge, skills, qualifications and/or business/self-employment experience. It is also not analysed for nationality/residence, i.e. UK/European or international student status.

The following criteria/definitions and anomalies were considered during analysis of the data generated:

- Project – this refers to the first two years of the Masters in Business and Enterprise programme.
- Programme – refers to the course in total and includes the stages at postgraduate level of: certificate; diploma; and masters.

- ESF beneficiaries – the initial data presented focuses on the two-year ESF-funded project/programme where the majority of the cohort was financially supported (fees paid) due to their eligibility to receive a bursary.
- Non-ESF beneficiaries – these students were either (a) not eligible to receive a bursary under the ESF project criteria and within the project timeframe (e.g., cohort 1–2); or (b) were enrolled outside of the project time frame (i.e. cohorts 3–5).
- Self-funded – those students (a) not in receipt of or eligible for an ESF bursary and therefore not an ESF beneficiary (cohorts 1–2); or (b) fees were paid for through personal or other funds (e.g. student loan, employer, other) and therefore are classed as a non-ESF beneficiary.
- Presentation of percentages – where possible, all percentages have been rounded up/down to the nearest whole number.

References

Beaver, G., & Carr, P. (2002). The enterprise culture: Understanding a misunderstood concept. *Journal of Strategic Change, 11*(2), 105–113.

Beaver, G., & Prince, C. (2004). Management, strategy and policy in the UK small business sector: A critical review. *Journal of Small Business and Enterprise Development, 11*(1), 34–39.

Bennis, W.G., & O'Toole, J. (2005). How business schools lost their way. *Harvard Business Review, 83*(5), 96–104.

Birch, D. (1979). The job creation process. Unpublished report. In *MIT Programme on Neighbourhood and Regional Change,* prepared for the Economic Development Administration, US Department of Commerce, Washington, DC.

Bjerke, B., & Hultman, C. (2002). *Entrepreneurial marketing the growth of small firms in the new economic era.* Cheltenham: Edward Elgar.

Callaghan, J. (1976). *Towards a national debate.* Speech delivered at Ruskin College, Oxford, 18 October.

Carson, C., Gilmore, A., & Grant, K. (2001). SME marketing in practice. *Marketing Intelligence and Planning, 9*(1), 6–11.

Co, M., & Mitchell, B. (2006). Entrepreneurship education in South Africa: A nationwide survey. *Education and Training, 48*(5), 348–359.

Cunningham, A.C. (1991). *Developing managers: A study of the training and educational needs of public enterprise managers.* Working paper prepared for the Economic Development Institute of the World Bank.

Deacon, J.H. (2008). *A study of the meaning and operation of the language for marketing in context.* PhD thesis, University of Ulster.

Department of Trade and Industry (DTI). (2000). *Excellence and opportunity – a science and innovation policy for the 21st century.* (White Paper, Cm 4814). London: HMSO.

Department of Trade and Industry (DTI). (2001). *Productivity in the UK: Enterprise and the productivity challenge.* London: HMSO.

Entrepreneurial Action Plan for Wales (EAP). (1999). *Offering a helping hand to future Welsh Stars – consultation document.* Cardiff: Welsh Development Agency.

European Union. (2003). *Green paper: Entrepreneurship in Europe.* Brussels: Commission of the European Communities.

Gibb, A., & Davis, L. (1990). In pursuit of frameworks for the development of growth models of the small business. *International Small Business Journal, 9*(1), 15–31.

Gibb, A.A. (1993). The enterprise culture and education: Understanding enterprise education and its links with small business, entrepreneurship and wider entrepreneurial goals. *International Small Business Journal, 11*(3), 11–34.

Giunipero, L.C., Denslow, D., & Eltantawy, R. (2005). Purchasing/supply chain management flexibility: Moving to an entrepreneurial skill set. *Industrial Marketing Management, 34* (6), 602–613.

Henry, C., Hill, F., & Leitch, C. (2005). Entrepreneurship education and training: Can entrepreneurship be taught? Part 1 and 2. *Education and Training, 47*(2/3), 98–111 and 158–169.

Herrmann, K., Hannon, P., Cox, J., Ternouth, P., & Crowley, T. (2008). *Developing entrepreneurial graduates: Putting entrepreneurship at the centre of higher education.* London: Council for Industry and Higher education (CIHE), National Council for Graduate Entrepreneurship (NGCE) and the National Endowment for Science, Technology and the Arts (NESTA).

Holland, J.L. (1994). Separate but unequal is better. In M.L. Savickas & R.W. Lent (Eds.), *Convergence in career development theories* (pp. 45–52). Palo Alto, CA: CPP Books.

Holliday, A. (2007). *Doing and writing qualitative research* (2nd ed.). London: Sage.

Hytti, U., & O'Gorman, C. (2004). What is enterprise education? An analysis of the objectives and methods of enterprise education programmes in four European countries. *Education and Training, 46*(1), 11–23.

Jack, S.L., & Anderson, A.R. (1999). Entrepreneurship education within the enterprise culture: Producing reflective practitioners. *International Journal of Entrepreneurial Behaviour and Research, 5*(3), 159–176.

Jamieson, I. (1984). Education for enterprise. In A.G. Watts & P. Moran (Eds.), *CRAC* (pp. 19–27). Cambridge, MA: Ballinger.

Jones, B., & Iredale, N. (2006). Developing an entrepreneurial life skills summer school. *Innovations in Teaching and Learning International, 43*(3), 233–244.

Jones, B., & Iredale, N. (2010). Enterprise education as pedagogy. *Education and Training, 52* (1), 7–19.

Jones, C., & English, J. (2004). A contemporary approach to entrepreneurship education. *Education and Training, 46*(8/9), 416–423.

Jones-Evans, D., Williams, W., & Deacon, J. (2000). Developing entrepreneurial graduates: An action learning approach. *Education and Training, 42*(4/5), 289–298.

Kauffman, S. (1993). *The origins of order: Self-organisation and selection in evolution.* New York: Oxford University Press.

Kirby, D. (2004). Entrepreneurship education: Can business schools meet the challenge? *Education and Training, 46*(8/9), 531–541.

Kuratko, D. (2005). The emergence of entrepreneurship education: Development, trends, and challenges. *Entrepreneurship Theory and Practice, 29*(5), 577–598.

Matlay, H. (2006). Researching entrepreneurship and education. Part 2: What is entrepreneurship education and does it matter? *Education and Training, 48*(8/9), 704–718.

Minniti, M., & Levesque, M. (2008). Recent developments in the economics of entrepreneurship. *Journal of Business Venturing, 23*(6), 603–612.

Osterman, K.F., & Kottkamp, R.B. (2004). *Reflective practice for educators* (2nd ed.). Thousand Oaks, CA: Sage.

Penrose, E. (1959). *The theory of the growth of the firm.* Oxford: Basil Blackwell.

Pittway, L., & Cope, J. (2007). Entrepreneurship education: A systematic review of the evidence. *International Small Business Journal, 25*(5), 479–510.

Rae, D. (2000). Connecting enterprise and graduate employability challenges to higher education culture and curriculum? *Education and Training, 49*(8/9), 605–619.

Romer, P. (1994). The origins of endogenous growth. *Journal of Economic Perspectives, 8* (1), 3–22.

Scase, R. (2007). *Global remix – the fight for competitive advantage.* London: Kogan Page.

Schumpeter, J.A. (1934). *The theory of economic development.* Cambridge, MA: Harvard University Press.

Stanworth, J., & Gray, C. (Eds.). (1991). *Bolton 20 years on: The small firm in the 1990s.* London: Chapman.

Stebbins, R. (2001). *Exploratory research in the social sciences.* Thousand Oaks, CA: Sage.

Storey, D., & Johnson, S. (1987). *Job generation and labour market change.* Basingstoke: Macmillan.

Taatila, V.P. (2010). Learning entrepreneurship in higher education. *Education and Training, 52*(1), 48–61.

Thurik, R., & Wennekers, S. (2004). Entrepreneurship, small business and economic growth. *Journal of Small Business and Enterprise Development, 11*(1), 140–149.

Timmons, G.A. (1999). *New venture creation: Entrepreneurship for the 21st century.* Boston, MA: Irwin/McGraw Hill.

Van Tassel-Baska, J. (1994). *Comprehensive curriculum for gifted learners* (2nd ed.). Boston, MA: Pearson.

Volkmann, C., Wilson, K.E., Mariotti, S., Rabuzzi, D., Vyakarnam, S., & Sepulveda, A. (2009). *Educating the next wave of entrepreneurs, unlocking entrepreneurial capabilities to meet the global challenges of the 21st century: A report of the global education initiative.* Paper presented at The World Economic Forum, Geneva, April.

Weik, K. (1995). What theory is not, theorizing is. *Administrative Science Quarterly, 40*, 385–390.

Whiteley, T. (1995). Enterprise in higher education – an overview from the Department for Education and Employment. *Education and Training, 37*(9), 4–8.

Planning for uncertainty: soft skills, hard skills and innovation

Elizabeth Chell and Rosemary Athayde

Kingston University, Kingston-upon-Thames, UK

The objective of this article is to explore how education for innovation of our young people may help develop an innovative mindset. The article develops the theoretical justification of a skills set which, it is argued, is fundamental for the development of an innovative mindset of young people, and consequently their personal development. We focus here on the qualitative work – focus groups and interviews with teaching staff and students aged 14–19 years – that informed our understanding of the five characteristics of this mindset; leadership, creativity, self-efficacy, energy and risk-propensity. The research attempted to capture the differences in context, constraints and school types and ethos that potentially shaped behavioural expression. Case studies based on types of school revealed detailed differences in context – regional, local and personal – that shaped students' engagement and their innovative behaviour in particular. The paper also reflects on teaching style, extracurricular opportunities for skills' development and student motivation to acquire an innovation skills set. The paper reflects on practical and policy implications of this work and identifies areas for further research.

Introduction

Since 2007 the global economy has been plunged into crisis and the financial future has become uncertain for many people. For young people this has affected their chances of employment, training, education and financial security. The scenario before us raises key issues for education as to how we should educate the next generation to cope with the aftermath of the current problem and the future which suggests global shifts in world power, continuing economic crises and a vast array of social problems trailing in its wake. People of all ages, colours and creeds face an abyss in which solutions are not evident and, where they exist, often lack substance or sustainability.

Previous government initiatives in the UK have attempted to address the problems of the time; especially relevant are those of the problems of the UK's international competitiveness and the development of its entrepreneurial and innovative potential. In these two crucial ways a platform has been set upon which we may build.

Debate has also been evident concerning education for the development of academic credentials and education and training in practical skills. Leitch (2006) and others have argued strongly for the need to develop practical skills. This call may be seen in a wider context of: (1) maintenance of the UK's competitiveness; (2) the employability of young people; (3) support for the UK's manufacturing base; and (4) the development of new innovative industrial sectors, thus lessening dependency on the financial sector.

Conventional employment pathways appear already to be being eroded for many young people, where academic qualifications alone are no longer sufficient to ensure a job for which the young person believes he or she has been trained. Already any work, part-time work or further training, have become the lesser goals for many young people.

Given this backdrop, we in education should ask ourselves what we might deliver to help young people to equip themselves better to secure jobs, or indeed to be effectively self-employed. This suggests that a skills agenda is no longer an option, but a necessary adjunct to the life chances and opportunities for young people coming through the system. It is timely that both staff and student should reflect on how young people's skills might be developed alongside an academic agenda.

In this article we aim to explore a basic skills agenda that will be feasible to deliver in schools cost-effectively and should better prepare our young people for a demanding future ahead.

The objective of this article is to explore how education for innovation of our young people may help. It aims to develop the theoretical justification of a basic skills set which, it is argued, is fundamental for the personal development of young people.

Conceptual framework

Human beings are highly skilled. One of the characteristics of a skill is that it is taken for granted (Polanyi, 1967). Once it is learnt, the actions that constitute the skill are carried out subconsciously. Indeed we may even cease to value the acquisition of the particular skill. When people think of skills they tend to think narrowly of practical down-to-earth activities involving tools or activities such as driving or riding a bicycle; sports, where hand-eye coordination or reaction times may be crucial; or drawing, where observation or precision may be useful skills. These examples of skills are not intellectual skills and draw on particular individual capabilities.

However, there are skills which also have an important cognitive content; they require judgement, assessment, decision-making, discernment and choice. Most professional judgments fall into this category, but so do the decisions of entrepreneurs and innovators. Hence, when we consider the basic skills set of such people, cognitive behaviour is fundamental (see Chell [2008] for a review and summary).

Usage of the terminology 'soft' and 'hard' skills is quite misleading. So-called 'hard' skills have a high knowledge and technical content, and it is essential that an incumbent has achieved a high level of competence in the particular knowledge domain if they are to be allowed to practice the skill (for example, a surgeon). 'Soft' skills in comparison are thought to be comparatively easy; they constitute behaviours, and are not thought to be conceptually difficult and may be acquired through experience. However, the successful execution of 'soft' skills is probably more challenging than once believed. This is not only due to the cognitive content of the skill, but also understanding of the context. Add to this the apparent fact that some skills (e.g. risk-taking) are not unidimensional and we have considerable behavioural complexity. In this article we focus on just five behavioural ('soft') skills and consider their relevance in entrepreneurship and innovation as applied to young people. However, they are relevant at the outset of the innovative process and do not include the implementation skills necessary for completion of the process.

Entrepreneurship and innovation commence with the germ of an idea. Imagination, understanding and the ability to develop the idea are fundamental to getting started. Consciously or not, disparate ideas need to be connected; an understanding of the direction of development is also required. This process is that of creative thinking. Creativity is not tied to the arts but can take place in any knowledge domain (Amabile, 1983). It is necessary but not sufficient for innovative entrepreneurship.

Several other cognitive skills also come into play. Having developed an idea, the innovator needs to be able to convince others of its worth; marshal arguments for its further development; and indeed see off rivals (Witt, 1998). The ability to exercise ideas-leadership as well as interpersonal and team leadership is essential to carry the developing opportunity forward (Vise, 2004).

Moreover, the innovator believes in his or her idea (Roddick, 1992; Gold, 1995) and is seen to display confidence and self-efficacy (Boyd & Vozikis, 1994). According to Bandura (1977, 1994), self-efficacy – the feelings of empowerment, self-confidence and self-assurance – is developed through a process of social learning. People observe others whom they regard as role models for the particular skill. Through imitation and mastery they gradually become more confident in their own abilities to execute a task successfully. Thus, such socio-cognitive skills are honed through experience; they are learnt behaviours which mean that training and education have a potentially powerful role to play.

Pursuit of an idea – some might say, a dream – requires energy. To be an effective innovative entrepreneur requires persistence, proactivity and drive (Chell, Haworth, & Brearley, 1991; Bateman & Crant, 1993). This level of mission carries the entrepreneur forward through tough times as well as through the often lengthy process of opportunity-testing, development and exploitation. Such purposeful behaviour requires conation; that is, recognition of the meaningfulness of the mission; cognition, involves thought and judgment about its worth; and, affect, the feelings that accompany the sense of achievement or otherwise (Robinson, Stimpson, Huefner, & Hunt, 1991; McClelland, 1961; Mischel & Shoda, 1998).

The social and economic context in which all this activity is taking place is fundamentally uncertain and decisions are taken in which there is an element of risk. How high that risk is will depend on a number of factors, not least the risk-propensity of the individual. How far are they prepared to go? What are the risks now and further down the line? Clearly judgement is again crucial. But there is evidence that people's risk-propensity varies considerably. Furthermore, risk-taking propensity may well be domain specific. In other words, a person may be prepared to take risks, say with their health (e.g. through drug, sex or alcohol abuse), but not with their money or their career (or vice versa) (Nicholson et al., 2005).

Research on risk-taking and young people has tended to focus on health, lifestyle and crime (Mitchell et al., 2001; Shaw, Caldwell, & Kleiber, 1996; Sweeting & West, 2003; Taylor, 2005). There is a dearth of research which focuses on young people's attitudes to financial risk-taking (Sjöberg & Engelberg, 2006). Even within a domain, it would appear that risk-taking propensity is not unidimensional (Nicholson et al., 2005; Chell & Athayde, 2009). Research suggests that there are: (1) sensation seekers; (2) risk/loss avoiders; (3) calculative risk-takers, who recognise inherent risks in what they are doing but take steps to reduce those risks; and (4) risk-adaptors or absorbers, who recognise the risks in what they do, but either naturally or through training learn to bear those risks. Insufficient research has been carried out as yet to support this typology of risk-taking.

Method

The method adopted includes a combination of qualitative design work – focus groups and interviews with young people across the target age span and teaching staff in a range of different types of school and college – and the development of an online measure of the basic innovative characteristics described above. To achieve this, accepted procedures for scale development with young people were followed which included reliability and validity testing (Cronbach, 1951, 1990; Nunnally & Bernstein, 1978; Athayde, 2009).

The research design for the qualitative study was that of embedded case studies (Yin, 1994). As a method of enquiry, case studies enable investigation of the phenomenon within its real-life context, often using multiple sources of evidence, which are triangulated in the analysis. The multiple case study design requires strong prior theoretical development and the generation of propositions to be tested through the cases. This method should not be confused with 'qualitative research', as the method adopted could be restricted to the generation of quantitative data only. Case studies investigate 'a contemporary phenomenon within its real-life context, especially when the boundaries between phenomenon and context are not clearly evident' (Yin, 1994, p. 13).

Unlike the laboratory experiment, where the context is controlled, or the survey, where it is often difficult to pick up sufficient contextual data, the multiple case studies enable one to deliberately cover contextual conditions. The pertinence of this to the current research is that cohorts of young persons (aged 14–16 years and 17–19 years) will be found, on the whole, in the contexts of different types of schools that may, additionally, have an inner city/rural context or a particular racial/ethnic mix. Hence, each type of school, college or university and its context will constitute 'multiple-experiments-in-context', from which analytical (as opposed to statistical) generalisations may be made. Moreover, the multiple case design permits experimentation, through comparative and pattern matching techniques. To assure quality for each criterion there are a variety of tactics that may be adopted (see Yin, 1994, pp. 33–38).

Unlike the single case study design that seeks to examine the unique or critical case, the multiple case study design identifies several cases and has the advantages of being more robust and compelling. Within a specific category or case (e.g. specialist school), replication logic is used to predict the same results for each school of that type. However, the issue of context appears where different categories of institution are assimilated into the design (e.g. city academies, sixth form colleges and so forth). This enables one to predict contrasting results for predictable reasons (e.g. the more academically inclined sixth form college compared with the more technical/practically oriented city academy).

There are a number of contextual conditions that are likely to result in variability in innovative activity between *types of school*. These we hypothesise to be: (1) practical versus academic orientation;[1] (2) location – inner city versus rural/semi-rural occupation; (3) teaching style; and (4) extracurricular activities. To explore these themes a series of focus groups was conducted with teachers and pupils. Thus, to avoid too much variety of institutions, we did not include university staff or students in this aspect of our method.[2]

The teacher focus groups at each school comprised six to eight teachers from different subject areas including: science; arts and humanities; sports; and on some occasions a teacher responsible for enrichment activities and pastoral care. In each case, the group was asked to discuss the five characteristics identified with innovative behaviour, to explain how pupils might be encouraged to develop these behaviours, and whether there were any constraints that limited opportunities for pupils to engage in these behaviours.

Pupils were asked to discuss the same topics as teachers and to describe where and how they were able to engage in these behaviours. To introduce the topics and put them into context, pupils were given examples of young entrepreneurs and winners of the recent Enterprising Young Brit awards to illustrate the characteristics of creativity, self-efficacy, risk-taking, energy and leadership. The focus groups included between eight and nine pupils from Years 10, 11 and, in some cases, the sixth form, and the age range was 14 to 18 year-olds.

The various stages of data collection and testing took place between October 2007 and December 2009. Project 1, comprising three surveys, is reported on the National Endowment for Science, Technology and the Arts (NESTA) website (http://www.nesta.org.uk). Project 2 comprised an evaluation exercise, which was reported internally to NESTA and is not reported here. Project 3 commenced in spring 2009 and comprised some revision of the measuring instrument, focusing in particular on the measures of energy and risk-propensity; the resultant instrument underwent two further tests on-line.

The types of schools include specialist schools in science, technology, arts, dance, music and drama, academies, and sixth form colleges; in Project 3 we included first-year students from four universities in England and Scotland. However, whilst we talked to some enterprise academics, we did not formally collect interview data with enterprise academics or students from the higher education sector.

The numbers of usable questionnaires from students surveyed in the 14–19 age groups are:

- Project 1 – Pilot 07, N = 239; MS1 08, N = 308; MS2 08, N = 811
- Project 3 – Pilot 09, N = 275; MS3 09, N = 708
- Overall total – 2,341

The students' profile included both males and females and a spread across ethnic minority groups.

We also discussed the project with a range of staff, and in particular sought to find out how staff might elicit innovative behaviour from their students and what the constraints might be. In this article we report qualitative interview data from staff and students within schools and sixth form colleges only. The interviews were exceptionally with one respondent (e.g. a head teacher) and most often we used the focus group format which allowed respondents to reflect on their own and each others' thoughts.

Results

The results of Project 1 are reported in Chell and Athayde (2009).

Current quantitative survey results

In similar vein, the quantitative survey results from Project 3 show good reliability and validity characteristics. #Cronbach alphas for each of the five innovative characteristics were: leadership = 0.853; self-efficacy = 0.804; creativity = 0.752; energy = 0.682; risk-propensity = 0.501; where the threshold of reliability is 0.7 (Cronbach, 1951; Nunnally & Bernstein, 1978). The measures also were found to have good predictive validity.

Interviews and qualitative analyses

Our brief included a focus on opportunities to develop innovative attitudes and skills within the formal and informal school/college day and also through extracurricular activities. Whilst the National Curriculum may be seen as a constraint, teaching style is important in enabling the teacher to draw out young people so that they are encouraged to express themselves innovatively, through assignments, class work, homework and through projects as appropriate. Formally, examinations may present a constraint where standards of achievement are held high. Schools and colleges vary in type, performance and ethos. Where engagement of students' interest is paramount, then the conditions for encouraging innovation exist; whereas a tight focus on the National Curriculum interpreted in an academic way may constrain experiential learning.

However, it is too easy to generalise and not take into account the complexity of subject specialisms, the quality of teaching and the vocational orientation of some subjects. Challenges in class facing many teachers could include a wide ability range, socially deprived students and students whose first (or even second) language was not English. Here, vocationally-oriented subjects such as the performing arts, music and media studies allow students to develop 'soft' skills. However, one of our schools which specialised in the performing arts and is based in a relatively affluent area of Hampshire also focused on the 'hard' skills – literacy, numeracy and analysis associated with A Level subjects. Where students were disaffected and uninterested in the academic route, the vocational route could provide engagement, as we found in a specialist technology school.

Managing the school life cycle requires a degree of balance to enable students to enjoy a subject and also to attain in it. National examinations and performance measures which emphasise attainment can limit the time for exploration of a subject outside the curriculum, though ways were found to achieve this in many of the schools and colleges we visited. In one college this was achieved through project work where the formative development of the student was emphasised over summative assessment. The use of theme days and enrichment weeks were also means of fostering a more creative and experiential approach to personal skills development and learning.

The vocational orientation, projects and activities pursued outside the curriculum and extracurricular activities not only engage students but help develop a 'can-do' attitude. Students that found it difficult to engage in class suddenly find something that they are able to do; this in itself is rewarding, but it also helps develop their self-confidence. Schools also use different systems of goal-setting, reward and praise to encourage aspiration and develop self-confidence.

While our sample of schools and colleges was relatively small, all seemed to encourage their pupils to participate in extracurricular activities. Many of these helped students to develop leadership skills and a sense of self-efficacy amongst other skills. There were many examples, such as the Duke of Edinburgh awards, St John's Ambulance, Army Cadets, Girl Guides, Young Enterprise, and being entered for competitions such as the Jack Petchy Foundation awards. As these teachers explained:

> Being involved and engaged gives the child a sense of control, thus developing their self confidence and self-efficacy.

> Students are freer to make more mistakes and learn from them; they can explore their own boundaries within limits.

> Going on trips and arranging external activities with light touch supervision can raise awareness of risks.

In the academies the extracurricular activities included sports clubs, drama, enterprise events (such as enterprise week), trips, exchanges and Duke of Edinburgh awards. However, there was some debate among teachers about how students could find time for these. Some had long school days, some students had outside commitments (for example, looking after younger siblings). So the extent that extracurricular activities can provide outlets for innovative behaviour depends on a range of factors including socio-economic background and family circumstances.

In the sixth form colleges there was a range of extracurricular activities on offer. However, in the London College it was felt that only vocational students benefited from these activities as they contributed towards their final qualification. Academic (A Level) students were too busy to take part, and would not gain 'points' that would enhance their qualifications. Also, teachers felt that it was easier for the vocational students to take risks:

> Low academic attainment by some pupils means they have 'nothing to lose', and so are more open to experimenting and taking risks.

One academy encouraged students to suggest initiatives and the result was an 'enterprise club'. The new academies obviously have new facilities in information and communication technologies (ICT), studios, theatre, video conferencing, design studios, and teachers hope that in future these will bear fruit. A business and enterprise focus in one academy led to a desire for innovative teaching and engagement with students; an attitude 'change' perceived to be important to generate innovative behaviour. As the head teacher explained:

> The enterprise agenda of the school provides the incentive and encouragement for new ideas towards teaching and extra-curricular activities.

One science specialist school had developed a virtual learning environment, which fostered the personal development of students, building self-efficacy and independent learning, energy and creativity skills. Teachers described this as a means of developing energy and self-efficacy via personal development and creativity and risk-taking via a number of cross-school collaborations. However, in practice this collaboration was perceived to present logistical and practical difficulties stemming from the need to cover the many objectives outlined in the National Curriculum.

Another barrier to innovation was assessment. Some teachers advocated more student-based self-assessment. Others argued that the adoption of ICT necessitated new forms of assessment.

In one academy a new integrated curriculum, based on themes, was anticipated to engender innovative behaviour in the future once it is embedded. In all the academies teachers felt that the early years offered more scope for innovative behaviour. However, at Key Stage 4, the requirement, assessments and content of subjects for examination were perceived to constrain innovation.

In all the academies the view was that grading, examinations and the National Curriculum restricted students' innovative behaviour. Students focused on exams rather than extracurricular activities; qualifications were perceived as a route to financial security and a better quality of life. Teachers suggested there is more scope for creativity and innovation in vocational courses; while A Level students are focused on examinations and exam technique. How the courses were taught was also perceived by teachers to have an impact on students' approach to risk. For instance, in one London sixth form college a teacher explains the disadvantages of the modular approach used in A Level courses compared to the more integrated vocational courses:

> Vocational students tend to stay together throughout the college day, developing a secure environment in which to take risks whereas A Level students' groups change according to subject.

It became clear, however, that some skills are nurtured far more than others. Whilst leadership, creativity, self-efficacy, motivation and engagement are being addressed, there appears to be a large gap in understanding risk and uncertainty. There does not seem to be provision for educating young people in this fundamental aspect of life and specifically of innovation.

There were some isolated instances of risk-taking in class which related to 'having a go' – experimenting and trying things out. But such a style of teaching evident in design technology would need to be exercised more widely for students to make the connections with a way of doing that facilitated skills' development for innovation. In discussion with students specifically about their understanding of risk-taking behaviour, this tended to be associated in their minds with their physical safety, for instance through sports activities – snorkelling, horse-riding, etc. – and academic achievement – making their grades – than anything to do with financial or economic risk-taking.

The emphasis generally was on developing students' self-confidence through personal interaction with pupils, including time spent with tutors, house systems, building trust and a 'safe' environment. In such cases teachers focused on how to make pupils feel 'safe' enough to take risks:

> [It is] important to balance risks; create an ethos in which the child is permitted to make mistakes but also to learn from them.

> Understanding that children fear failure and therefore finding ways to assess and support children so that they do not develop a sense of having failed.

Presentations, peer teaching, mentoring younger pupils and cross-curricular activities were all used to develop confidence and trust. ICT was seen as an important resource in the development of personally directed learning. In the lower achieving colleges in London the emphasis was on creating a safe environment where students were encouraged to participate. In the Hampshire sixth form colleges there was more scope for independent learning and students were encouraged to develop problem-solving skills. Once again, socio-economic backgrounds were seen to have implications for what was taught and how it was delivered.

Case studies

Embedded case studies were analysed based on the contextual themes that were identified. There are a number of contextual conditions that are likely to result in variability in innovative activity between *types of school*, comprising: practical versus academic orientation; location – inner city versus rural/semi-rural occupation; teaching style; extracurricular activities; and opportunities created by the school to encourage innovation. To explore these themes a series of focus groups was conducted with teachers and pupils, which allowed for mature reflection on these issues raised.

The London schools included a city academy, international business and enterprise college, with sixth form, and a specialist school in science, maths and ICT. In Hampshire the sample comprised one large further education college with a wide catchment area in the south-east including the Isle of Wight, and a large secondary school in a semi-rural, wealthy location, whence many people commute to London. The demographic profile of students was very different in these two regions.

London schools are culturally and academically diverse. The city academy has pupils from 65 countries who speak 34 languages. English is spoken as an additional language by 75%. A higher than average proportion has special educational needs. The specialist science school also has higher than average cultural diversity and has a wide range of academic ability, from high achievers to pupils achieving well below the national average at GCSE level. In contrast the schools in Hampshire had a more homogeneous profile, which comprised students with mainly white British backgrounds, with few special educational needs; typically high achieving pupils with generally high aspirations. For instance, pupils at a Hampshire sixth form college described their high aspirations. Some were involved in music bands and a sixth form boy had started his own recording studio in his bedroom. Another 16-year-old talked about the financial rewards from his musical pursuits:

> I do a lot of music stuff outside school though I have limited it a bit now because I have my GCSEs. I'm in quite a few different bands and some of them have been set up by me. I did a gig with my brother and his friend and we were paid quite a lot of money. Then there is another band and we made a CD and we made quite a lot of money doing that.

These demographic differences had implications for what the schools aim to achieve and the way in which they go about achieving these aims. The Hampshire schools were geared towards achieving high grades at GCSE and A levels, while enrichment activities also aimed high in subjects such as drama, music and dance. In contrast, the London schools aimed at improving academic standards and ensuring pupils left school with the basics to enable them to find work or go on to vocational training. There was a small cohort of high achievers in each of the London schools, where the focus was on high grades.

In one inner city school there was a strong focus on vocational skills through the introduction of a wide range of vocational courses and qualifications. The school profile offered special challenges. Over half of the pupils have English as a second language. There are significant minorities of 'looked after' children and pupils from refugee or asylum-seeking families. Teaching styles adopted in these more vocationally oriented schools tended to promote friendship and emotional support. Teachers reflected on the impression that some students did not want to go home at the end of the day because they received much more support at school than at home; such teachers work on Saturdays and Sundays to meet demand. This support is also demonstrated through etiquette such as shaking hands and greeting each other warmly in corridors and in the school grounds. Students disliked teachers who 'lectured' or 'talked all the time' and they preferred to take part in activities. They also preferred to use computers rather than having to write by hand. Assessment was focused on presentations and posters rather than essay writing.

Involvement in extracurricular activities was influenced, and constrained, by a number of factors. The demographic mix of pupils was thought by teaching staff to have an impact on levels of confidence; for example, it was noted that girls from some ethnic minority groups often lacked confidence. Staff ascribed this to a 'culture of diffidence from their parents'. Another demographic factor was age. The teachers reported young pupils were more likely to be open to 'making a fool of themselves', whereas the older ones were more 'cool' and worried about how their peers perceived them. These same demographic factors were associated with low risk-taking, especially among Asian boys.

The other crucial demographic factor influencing innovative behaviour was parents' occupations and aspirations. The teachers noted that many of the students in inner city schools were ill-equipped to come up with new ideas or manage projects. They claimed students were more comfortable waiting for the school to offer them a trip or extracurricular activity as opposed to organising it. One example was two students who started to raise money to build a school in Africa, but later stopped due to the challenges.

Many students displayed little evidence of participating in extracurricular activities. This was attributed to the long school days. One girl provided details of how her personal life beyond the academy influenced the extent to which she could engage in extracurricular activities:

> My mum is a single parent and with GCSEs, I still try to do sport, I like basketball and stuff like that, but I often miss practice 'cos I have to go home to cook dinner for my younger brother and sister, and look after them like.

Thus, these experiences of pupils in inner city schools contrasted with rural schools, where students from more affluent backgrounds were more confident in engaging in a range of activities.

Discussion

This programme of work has involved both quantitative and qualitative research methods to assess five basic innovative characteristics of young people. The findings from the quantitative study are promising, but the purpose of this paper is to outline the qualitative interview and focus group work which revealed so much about both teacher and student attitudes towards innovative behaviour and the five characteristics that we identified as fundamental. The attitude to inserting innovative behaviour and the development of characteristics in young people that would facilitate it was shown to be restricted by a number of factors, not least of which was the curriculum and the ethos of the institution toward an academic or vocational orientation.

The lack of any formal teaching of economics or financial management in the schools and colleges we sampled meant that any understanding of such issues would most likely reflect the interest and intelligence of the student and/or his or her socio-economic background. This situation is reflected more broadly across schools and colleges nationwide. Some of the older students (especially first-year university students) and students participating in extracurricular activities such as Young Enterprise or the Duke of Edinburgh awards may have developed a more finely tuned understanding of economic and financial risk-taking, but this is difficult to know. Certainly when we disaggregated the risk-taking propensity data and re-analysed it by age, the Cronbach alphas for the older students were higher (for example, for 18-year-olds, where $N = 107$ students, the Cronbach alpha was 0.711 across all nine items). This suggests that we need to do more to understand young people of different age groups' level of awareness, and depth of knowledge, of risk-taking propensity. We also need to build a measure that truly reflects different types of risk-takers, thus revealing its multi-dimensional substructure.

Hence, further research should include qualitative design work around the notion of different risk types in the economic and financial domain. We should draw on young people by age group in an attempt to understand in detail their risk-taking propensity, in particular taking into consideration context and situations that may act as triggers to risk-taking. We also should consider whether students in the younger age groups (14–15 years) respond differently to economic risk-taking stimuli. If so, are they too young, and lacking both experience and self-awareness, to respond with any consistency to a measure of risk-taking propensity? We should identify a sample of schools where some financial management is taught to young people and categorise schools accordingly. This dimension should be cross-tabulated with the vocational versus academic focus and mission of the school or college.

Outside of the National Curriculum there are opportunities for students of all ages to acquire skills through heuristic and social learning. Understanding money, household management, savings accounts, debt and, say, gambling are just some themes that might be pursued in schools to introduce the student to notions of risk. These topics lend themselves to games and project work, and should form a prerequisite to enterprise projects. Developing such an understanding would also improve some students' numeracy and analytical skills in a fun way.

Some people would refer to the five characteristics underpinning initial innovative behaviour that we have identified as 'soft' skills. However, as already intimated, 'soft' is not necessarily easy. The components of the skills include a knowledge- and belief-set, as well as the ability to discern and make appropriate choices, given understanding of the context. This rather more complex definition of a behavioural skill is essential in our view for young people to develop and execute these behavioural skills successfully. Furthermore, from a practical perspective, for young people to acquire these skills, the skill content and focus must be meaning-ful. As such, this enables them to assimilate the requisite behaviours, and translate and direct their behaviour towards a set of goals which they want to achieve. Doing so gives them positive feelings towards the activity and makes success especially rewarding.

A practical implication of this is that young people should be given opportuni-ties to exercise and develop an innovative mindset and the five associated skills in contexts that are meaningful and chosen by them. This allows students to reflect on behaviours, contexts and consequences of chosen actions and activities in concrete terms. Moreover, the barriers identified in discussion with both staff and students clearly need to be addressed. The problems highlighted in respect of assessment, for example, are nationwide and require a considered debate and reflection beyond the boundaries of any particular school or college. It is clear, however, that a debate is needed amongst the profession.

However, there was some light thrown on the problem. In one academy a new integrated curriculum, based on themes, was anticipated to engender innovative behaviour in the future once it is embedded. In all the academies teachers felt that the early years offered more scope for innovative behaviour. At Key Stage 4 the requirement assessments and content of subjects for examination were perceived to constrain innovation. However, there is also an issue of maintaining that focus when, in later years, there is a switch to achievement through national examina-tions.

Thus, in all the schools visited the view was that grading, examinations and the National Curriculum restricted students' innovative behaviour. This was because students focused on examination results and grades rather than extracurricular activ-ities; qualifications were perceived as a route to financial security and a better qual-ity of life. Teachers suggested there is more scope for creativity and innovation in vocational courses; A level students are focused on exams and exam technique.

However, if government and educationalists are to address such a skills issue seriously, then reflection on how to embed skills development in young people will be necessary in a detailed way, by, for example, deconstructing the syllabus for any particular discipline and focusing on how a particular theme may be communicated not only in an engaging way but in a way that allows for practical reflection. In the more vocationally oriented schools and colleges, and indeed subjects, arguably some headway has been made in this regard, as evidenced from student commen-tary. But there is still a long way to go if our sample is anything to go by. More-over, the research also implies various practical possibilities for teachers and lecturers in secondary and further education. With the loosening of the National Curriculum and the continued expansion of the academies, there are more opportu-nities for staff and students to engage in reflecting on the nature of skills for inno-vation and entrepreneurship. This should increase over the current government education policy. Potentially the approach has implications for the employability of young people. To a large extent the development of skills for innovation and entre-preneurship has already happened in higher education institutions over the last dec-ade, although there may be a case made for its further expansion.

People might argue about what should constitute the five skills or suggest that the set should be expanded to include other skills that they deem as, or perhaps more, important. Just as literacy and numeracy skills are important for the young person to acquire, we believe that the five basic skills for innovation are also fundamental. Being a successful innovator or entrepreneur requires a considerably larger skills set (see Chell, 2008, p. 211), so as the young person takes steps towards the goal of developing an idea, spotting an opportunity or pursuing self-employment, then it will be essential for him or her to acquire further skills. But such a discussion is beyond the scope of this article.

We have highlighted additional research that is needed to develop the measuring instrument further. There are also practical implications of this research for which the ability to discern and measure basic innovative skills of young people is just the start-point. Our work with NESTA will give young people who have completed the final version of the questionnaire a report and guidance that will be helpful in his or her self-development. The tool may be used to focus discussion around career pathways and choices available to students, such as the nature of any further training or personal development and choice of further/higher education, employment or self-employment options. The increased awareness should help students to consciously improve their skills and take better-informed decisions about their future.

Implicit in the above discussion are policy implications at various levels: school to address and deliver such basic skills' agenda as identified; further and higher education to expand the career pathways and the skills development of students for self-employment, innovation and entrepreneurship. This has profound implications for the relevant government departments in education and also skills.

Acknowledgements

We would like to thank NESTA for its generous support in the development of this work. We would also like to thank all the teachers and students who took part in the projects that produced the current findings. Finally we would like to thank anonymous reviewers for their constructive comments.

Notes

1. Whilst schools of all types are required to deliver the National Curriculum, the difference between schools is the context and structure that may affect the nature of the delivery e.g. city academies are based on public private partnerships, which should present more opportunities for the expression of practical innovative behaviour. Whereas, for example, sixth form colleges focus rather more on the technical aspects of the discipline and as such may present *fewer* opportunities for the expression of innovative behaviour.
2. To boost the number of 19-year-old students in our sample we used first-year university students.

References

Amabile, T.M. (1983). *The social psychology of creativity*. New York: Springer.
Athayde, R. (2009). Measuring enterprise potential in young people, *Entrepreneurship Theory and Practice,* March, 481–500.
Bandura, A. (1977). *Social learning theory*. Englewood Cliffs, NJ: Prentice Hall.
Bandura, A. (1994). Self-efficacy. In: V.S. Ramachaudran (Ed.), *Encyclopaedia of human behaviour,* Vol. *4*, (pp. 71–81). New York: Academic Press.
Bateman, T.S., & Crant, J.M. (1993). The proactive component of organisational behaviour – a measure and correlates. *Journal of Organisational Behaviour, 14*, 103–118.
Boyd, N.G., & Vozikis, G.S. (1994). The influence of self-efficacy on the development of entrepreneurial intentions and actions. *Entrepreneurship Theory & Practice, 19*, 63–77.

Chell, E. (2008). *The entrepreneurial personality — a social construction* (2nd ed.). Hove: Routledge.

Chell, E., & Athayde, R. (2009). *The identification and measurement of innovative characteristics of young people*. London: NESTA.

Chell, E., Haworth, J.M., & Brearley, S. (1991). *The entrepreneurial personality: concepts, cases & categories*. London: Routledge.

Cronbach, L.J. (1951). Coefficient alpha and the internal structure of tests. *Psychometrika, 16*(3), 297–334.

Cronbach, L.J. (1990). *Essentials of psychological testing* (5th ed.). New York: HarperCollins.

Gold, J. (1995). *Good vibrations*. London: Pavilion.

Leitch, Lord S. (2006). *Prosperity for all in a global economy: World class skills*. London: HM Treasury.

McClelland, D.C. (1961). *The achieving society*. Princeton, NJ: D. Van Nostrand.

Mischel, W., & Shoda, Y. (1998). Reconciling processing dynamics and personality dispositions. *Annual Review of Psychology, 49*, 229–258.

Mitchell, R., Crawshaw, P., Bunton, R., & Green, E. (2001). Situating young people's experiences of risk and identity. *Health Risk & Society, 3*(2), 217–233.

Nicholson, N., Soane, E., Fenton-O'Creevy, M., & Williams, P. (2005). Personality and domain specific risk-taking. *Journal of Risk Research, 8*(2), 157–176.

Nunnally, J.C., & Bernstein, I.H. (1978). *Psychometric theory*. New York: McGraw-Hill.

Polanyi, M. (1967). *The tacit dimension*. London: Routledge.

Robinson, P.B., Stimpson, J.C., Huefner, J.C., & Hunt, H.K. (1991). An attitude approach to the prediction of entrepreneurship. *Entrepreneurship Theory & Practice, 15*, 41–52.

Roddick, A. (1992). *Body and soul*. London: Vermillion.

Shaw, Susan M., Caldwell, Linda L., & Kleiber, Douglas A. (1996). Boredom stress and social control in the daily activities of adolescents. *Journal of Leisure Research, 28*(4), 274–292.

Sjöberg, L., & Engelberg, E. (2006). *Attitudes to economic risk-taking, sensation-seeking and values of business students specialising in finance*. (SSE/EFI Working Paper Series in Business Administration No 2006: 3). Stockholm: School of Economics.

Sweeting, H., & West, P. (2003). Young people's leisure and risk-taking behaviours: Changes in gender patterning in the West of Scotland during the 1990s. *Journal of Youth Studies, 6*(4), 391–412.

Taylor, A. (2005). It's for the rest of your life: The pragmatics of youth career decision making. *Youth and Society, 36*(4), 471–503.

Vise, D.A. (2004). *The Google story*. London: Pan.

Witt, U. (1998). Imagination and leadership – the neglected dimension of evolutionary theory of the firm. *Journal of Economic Behaviour and Organisation, 35*, 161–177.

Yin, R.K. (1994). *Case study research* (2nd ed.). Thousand Oaks, CA: Sage.

Bank advisors working with contradiction: meeting the demands of control through reflective learning

Yngve Antonsen, Odd Arne Thunberg and Tom Tiller

Department of Education, University of Tromsø, Norway

This study of a Norwegian bank's strategic learning initiatives is based on theory about reflective learning and external constraints on learning. Its main aim is to investigate how the practice of reflective learning among advisors who provide customer service is influenced by new institutional demands, strategic learning initiatives and senior management in an organisation using the Balanced Scorecard. The empirical data were derived from 40 qualitative interviews, eight two-day focus groups and observation of 35 learning activities. Grounded theory was used to analyse the consistency or contradictions between organisational strategy and the understanding of employees about learning activities at work. In addition 2284 registered learning activities recorded by Bank employees on a Balanced Scorecard were analysed. Empirical findings indicate that the management's new top-down strategy for learning in the organisation – 'Best Customer Practice' (recording information about and accounting for learning) when combined with a new institutional demand for authorization and training – has a controlling function that contradicts the organisation's own rhetoric about promoting reflective learning among the employees. Employees value reflective learning arising from customer relations as it improves motivation and customer service in general. The broader may promote top-management control that constrains the contribution by employees of new ideas, based on reflection about their work, for improving the quality of the services that they provide.

Introduction

The demands and expectations for management to direct and control employees' work are now increasing in modern organizations (Radnor & Barnes, 2007). At the same time, organizations need their employees to initiate development and innovation to create long-term sustainability. This implies that the learning initiatives experienced by employees in organizations are connected to control of work or expected to promote new ideas, or both. This study of a Norwegian bank investigates how the use of strategic learning initiatives by senior management relates to employees' reflective learning from customer service. The context of the study is Norway, a country that receives top rating on socio-economic factors such as democracy, education and competence development in working life.

Theories about learning and change in organizations emphasize learning through reflection as centrally important for improving employees' work performance and customer service (Boud, Cressey, & Docherty, 2006). Schön's (1987) theory suggests that when employees learn from situations such as customer service, this learning can be seen as an interplay between the actual meeting, the 'action', reflection on the action and an analysis of new possibilities. Reflective learning involves thinking critically and creatively about the situation and 'is identified with a potential for change, as it questions key variables instead of just accepting and repeating a given body of knowledge' (Jarvis, Halford, & Griffin, 2003, p. 70). This requires employees to assess opinions, theories and practice from various positions and perspectives in order to assure quality (Dewey, 1991). Such processes may give rise to new alternatives to established organizational routines based on a more dynamic relationship between routines and reflection. Fenwick's (2008) review criticizes workplace learning research because it fails to pay critical attention to the importance of the power of management in promoting reflective learning in organizations.

Røvik (2007) reveals how new management systems, and especially the balanced scorecard (Kaplan & Norton, 1996), have become prescriptions for shaping modern organizations to pursue efficiency and are applied in many organizations at the same time. The scorecard is designed so that senior managers develop a predefined top-down strategic plan that directly influences how work tasks, both simple and complex, are performed and rewarded. Research on the use of the balanced scorecard reveals that this system strengthens senior management control by micromanaging in detail the work tasks of employees (Paranjape, Rossiter, & Pantano, 2006). Such top-down organizing of work tasks and methods is criticized because it decreases employees' opportunity to influence and participate in decisions about their own work (Voelpel, Leibold, & Eckhoff, 2006). Hierarchies in organizations tend to weaken opportunities for employees to reflect critically in order to improve their current practice (Argyris & Schön, 1996). Nilsen's (2007) study of a bank proposes that the use of the balanced scorecard and 'top-down strategies for learning' are tools for promoting employees obedience to authority. The business tradition of basing objectives on the volume of sales and services has been transferred to the financial sector and to banks. This contrasts sharply with the principles of reflective learning that serves to promote human growth by allowing learners to make personal choices (Jarvis et al., 2003).

Advisors in banks all over the world have been blamed for greed during the financial crisis of 2008. In banking organizations, central and local rules and credit routines are necessarily requirements for handling customers and assets. The mandatory New Norwegian Authorization Initiative for Advisors aims to ensure high-quality customer service by introducing and raising knowledge of ethical standards for customer relations and meetings. However, this study questions how senior management with the use of strategic learning initiatives and new institutional demands influences the practice of reflective learning among advisors who provide customer service.

This case study formed part of a four year research project on workplace learning in a traditional bank with more than 800 employees located in more than 80 departments of various sizes in Norway. The bank is highly driven, with very good profits and a top international 'A' Fitch Rating. The management system – the balanced scorecard – has been used as a recipe for maximizing the bank's profit since

2002. The senior management learning strategy aiming to improve customer service involves obligatory learning activities where two or more advisors share their knowledge and experience. In order to achieve a bonus, six learning sessions per month, each of 30 minutes, have to be registered by advisors as an indicator in the balanced scorecard. The written directives specify that these shared learning initiatives should not contain instruction, lectures or information. These initiatives aimed to increase employees' reflective learning in the bank.

Reflective learning from customer service

In this section we argue that employee's reflective learning from customer relations may be a tool for employee empowerment as well as meeting the organizational demands for control and efficiency. Schön (1987) distinguishes between the expert and the reflective practitioner. Experts are expected to know the answers even in uncertain situations. They signal that they know more than customers as a result of their expertise and ability to distance themselves from problems. In the professional meetings such experts are polite and sympathetic to clients but expect acquiescence from the customers. The reflective practitioner however does not necessarily have all the answers in uncertain situations. In meetings between the reflective practitioner and customers, they may both contribute information and knowledge and have to build mutual respect of each other's knowledge facilitated by the practitioner. In order to ensure high-quality customer meetings, reflective practitioners must also possess integrity and freedom that empowers them to solve problems that arise (Ellström, 2001). Hochschilds' (2003) empirical study confirms that face-to-face situations comprise the most significant learning experience for all involved. In situations where employees receive positive confirmation from customers, this can form a particularly solid basis for reflective learning. The quality of human encounters is crucial for reflective learning, motivation, well-being and self-image. Schön (1987) claims that reflection may contribute to self-knowledge and consciousness-raising about one's own knowledge. Ellström (2001) argues that such metacognitive knowledge is developed when the individual is aware of his or her limitations and strengths. Reflective work promotes knowledge, skills, self-confidence and motivation among individuals. Edmondson's (1999) study from learning in teams emphasizes psychological safety, trust and responsibility between members as the most important factors for facilitating critical questioning and reflection. Giving employees the opportunity for co-determination at work appears to be important in promoting learning among individuals and organizations.

Nonaka and Takeuchi (1995) express the importance of using reflective learning to identify and conceptualize tacit knowledge in organizations. For example, when the employees' own tacit knowledge about advising customers is articulated and conceptualized, it can be transferred to other colleagues. Such learning from experience is not an entirely simple process because work situations vary and are difficult to identify and analyse during a busy working life. Through distancing ourselves from the immediacy of practice, we can discover individual and collective experiences, allowing us to regulate, correct and change our practice. Varied and diverse reflection on practice can help prevent a uniform approach to task performance (Michel & Wortham, 2009). Thus, Giddens (1990) argues that reflection may contribute to creativity and innovation in working life, which is important in the competition for customers in a rapidly changing world.

An organizational strategy that promotes reflective learning and communication between customers, employees and senior management is crucial for quality assurance. However, individual learning and reflection alone are not enough to develop organizations. If the strategic learning initiatives in practice do not support learning from customer relations, then reflective learning from experience will falter.

Possible constraints for reflective learning

In working life when the pressure for efficiency increases, time for employees' learning through reflecting on work experiences is eroded (Giddens, 1990; Senge, 1999). Financial organizations in particular are working in a global market where the demands for profit have been increased also during the financial crisis of 2008 (Krugman, 2009). Hackman and Wageman (2005) argue that three combined key factors underpin team (in our case the team comprises advisors and office manager) performance of work tasks:

(1) The level of effort from the collective team to solve the work task;
(2) The suitability of the team's work methods or performance strategies for the tasks; and
(3) The sum and utilization of knowledge and skills that contribute to the team's execution of the task.

Hackman & Wageman (2005, p. 41) further argue that team level constraints limit office managers' and employees' opportunities to influence their own daily practice. For example, having few potential customers, or lacking relevant equipment may hinder efforts by employees to increase sales.

Also, performance strategies that use procedures, manual and technological, to specify in detail the methods to be used in work tasks hinder the potential of office managers and employees to influence and improve how work tasks are performed. In a review article Paranjape et al. (2006) explain that the balanced scorecard management system aims to increase efficiency through stronger senior management control. It is a top-down strategy guided by a rationalist economic perspective. The balanced scorecard is designed to convert the organization's strategic plan into effectively performed and rewarded work tasks (Kaplan & Norton, 1996) by counting and controlling the implementation of all work tasks and sales demands designed by management (Nilsen 2007). The senior managers have the power to define and make demands to which others must choose whether or not to conform. Intangible and tacit work practices are easily overlooked in organizations when management systems and models of economic organizations assume strong control over information, meetings and action (Nørreklit 2003). It is easy to conclude that using the balanced scorecard creates more operational rules, procedures and rigidity (Paranjape et al., 2006).

As senior managers really matter in promoting reflective learning, a destructive leader may hinder learning in an organization, and even well-regarded leaders are not always able to improve and affect the work of employees and office managers (Hackman & Wageman, 2005). Mintzberg, Ahlstrand and Lampel (1998) argue that the most important work of senior managers is strategic development because it directs and focuses the contribution of employees and office managers to organizational production and development. Senior managers have central responsibility for organizational learning that involves implementing and change in organizational strategies and routines (Argyris & Schön, 1996).

On the other hand, when the senior management using the balanced scorecard decides to change manuals that detail work tasks, employees' learning may also be seen as matter of making only a simple adjustment to regulate performance (Argyris & Schön, 1996). Participants may become disillusioned when administration and organizational strategies obstruct development. Critical participants who suggest new solutions and improvements in their organization may be seen as disloyal to management. Without room for such criticism, they may find themselves vulnerable or isolated, especially if only a few employees are critical of operations or power (Hackman & Wageman, 2005).

Hackmann and Wageman (2005) further emphasize three contextual constraints that influence team performance in organizations:

(1) Organizations have a main noble purpose that motivates members to work hard and increase their effort to help other people independently of managers' instructions. Bank advisors give financial help to customers by means of loans, insurance and savings.

(2) Strong institutional laws and regulations specify how organizations should operate, and these regulate how bank advisors should perform their tasks to prevent fraud and economic crime.

(3) The labour market influences how banks promote competence and learning among advisors and office managers. Learning opportunities at work may increase employees' motivation for working in a bank. Learning may also increase the control of how employees deal with work tasks. To facilitate development we argue that banks also have to provide occasions for employees to learn from each other by means of reflective learning. Argyris and Schön (1996) conclude that reflective learning, without opportunities to change practices, provides few learning gains for employee and organization. Research indicates that the management must aid reflection on practice and must give up power if employees are to exercise influence (Michel & Wortham, 2009). Vince (2002) argues that inclusion and integration are keys to enhanced collaborative critical reflection, where everybody participates in the process even though they have different functions in the organization. Three major constraints appear to be: insufficient time or reflection; insufficient motivation to learn through reflection on significant working life moments/ encounters; and having insufficient influence to put such learning to good use in further improving performance.

Methods and analysis

The following section introduces the sources of our qualitative and quantitative data and our method of analysis. The qualitative materials were collected and analysed over a 30-month period. Thirty-two customer advisors and eight office managers were interviewed. These informants of various ages, length of service and both genders were randomly selected from five different branches of the bank. In these 30–60-minute interviews we asked open-ended questions in order to have a constructive dialogue. The use of semi-structured interviews allowed the researcher to let the interview flow and follow up leads and information from the advisors and office managers. This enabled us to explore the learning of customers, colleagues and the bank in general. Two researchers attended, both separately and together, 35 learning activities in five departments over a two-year period. To enhance the empirical evidence, eight, two-day focus groups were conducted in which three researchers and an average of 10 office managers volunteered to discuss and analyse the bank's learning challenges (Wilkinson, 2004). In general, a good level of trust and interaction between office managers, advisors and researchers led to a rich set of empirical data. All the data were transcribed, in addition to written summaries from 25 learning activities. We used the data analysis software NVivo 8 (Bazeley, 2007) with the purpose of categorizing grounded data to understand how the employees understood, agreed and differed about strategies and customer learning in the bank (Glaser & Strauss, 1967). In the resulting varied material about learning, all similar statements were first openly coded into categories based on the data. Thereafter these categories were employed, clarified and confirmed through use of field notes, memo writing and discussions between researchers. The number of categories increased by building 'trees' of categories to capture order in the data. The analysis reveals four strategic and institutional learning initiatives that were used to develop customer service by the bank over a three-year period: 'Best Customer Practice'; information and accounting of learning activities; authorization; and training. Advisors and office managers valued learning from customer relations as most important for improving their own work tasks. This contradicted their statements about the senior management's strategic learning initiatives.

We used an overview of all employees' recorded learning activities completed from January 2008 to June 2009, a total of 2,284 entries. These records gave us systematic information about what kinds of learning activities are most salient in the organization. Some caveats about this overview process are needed: the high amount of short and possibly imprecise descriptions contained in the entries might produce a potential self-reporting bias; employees may have copied each other's entries while completing the required records even if they had learned different content; the records also lack a precise timetable; different learning content is often summed up in only one recorded learning activity, and duplicated entries are also evident; 7% of the original material lacked descriptions and was taken out of the analysis; and, finally, there may have been unrecorded learning activities. The strength of the analytical work is that two researchers took part both in the data collection in different levels of the organization and in the categorization (researcher triangulation). Also, the inter-rater reliability is confirmed as the researchers both found consensus between both the quantitative material and the recorded entries.

The bank's priorities and context

The rhetoric of the bank in this case study corresponds to modern discourses of working life and concepts such as 'learning', 'team work', 'learning organization', are evident in its strategic planning documents. 'The bank is a learning organization, which actively develops employee's knowledge, skills and attitudes to solve the customers' requirements'.

As early as in 1992, the bank began to focus on building long-term, high-quality customer relations. The stated vision and ambition in 2009 was to be 'close to and competent for' all customers, and thus to provide the best advice based on local accessibility, relations and knowledge. But surveys of customer satisfaction indicate perceptions that competence is less than in competing banks. The challenge for the past 17 years has been to strengthen customer relations, at a time when on-line banking and automated teller machines have reduced the need for face-to-face contact between advisors and customers. Modern banking has become more efficient and has reduced the need for expensive face-to-face transactions (Flohr Nielsen & Preuthun Pedersen, 2003; Nilsen 2007). When orders and requests from the customers are carried out automatically, both contact and costs are reduced.

This bank, like other banks, is organized hierarchically and characterized by top-down management, as all our respondents confirmed in the analysis:

> The hierarchy in a bank is strong. If the senior management asks for a report from everybody within a week, all will provide one! (Office manager in a focus group)

Our analysis reveals that senior management emphasizes the need for increased efficiency, change and adaptation to the market. In a very hectic round of everyday customer work, employers and managers are challenged to increase profitability through a focus on sales, advice, control, reports, prognoses and information. These new demands, in addition to lack of personnel, increase stress among the advisors from all the five branches in the bank. A common quote from our interviews is:

> We have had large level of stress over time because of lack of personnel. (Advisor in interview)

This finding about the advisors' lack of time was also confirmed by all office managers in the focus groups.

The advisor's voice: learning from customer contact and the constraints of credit routines

The advisors' most important source of motivation and energy for learning comes from customer contact. All advisors emphasized in interviews that good customer relations are important for well-being, job satisfaction and professional pride. The advisors are aware that they are seen as significant in the life of the customers:

> I feel that I can contribute something. I like having people around. No two customer meetings are the same, and this is why I have stuck it out for so long. I simply don't take sick leave, because I feel responsibility for the customers. The customers are loyal to me, and I am loyal to them. (Advisor in interview)

Positive feedback from customers usually comes verbally, directly to the advisors or to the management. But feedback from customers may also come in the form of visible actions such as sending flowers and candy. On such occasions, the positive message is also spread to colleagues through a symbolic gift which is left on the desk, or by means of discussion in the lunch room.

All interviewed advisors and office managers emphasized that knowledge of how to advise is developed through experience. The advisors learn sales techniques and relationship-building in practice, through customer contact. Being able to see each individual customer and to find good, flexible solutions based on the needs of the customer and the requirements of the bank gives the advisor a sense of competence and of making a difference in the customer's life. At a time when products of banks are becoming more and more similar and competition intensifies, advisors focus on the importance of this knowledge gained from customer contact. A majority of advisors also emphasized that flexibility in adapting solutions to problems provides a competitive advantage for the bank. This scope for influence and action has been an important factor for working in the bank.

Decisions of greatest significance are made by senior management to maximize profit and reduce losses. The interviewed advisors, who knew their customers well, revealed that they had to adhere increasingly to new credit or sales instructions and felt squeezed between customer loyalty and loyalty to the system:

> You have customers that make one million kroner a year. They have huge cash assets, but they may have problems when the interest rate increases because of high expenditure. The simulated figures do not reveal inter-human aspects, such as how you are as a person and your willingness to pay your debts. But customers with a low income and a strong willingness to pay may be more valuable for the bank in the long term. (Advisor in interview)

New complicated credit manuals were sometimes unclear and vague, with the result that customer credit applications may be rejected when advisors present them to the management. It is difficult for an advisor who knows the customer well to reject him or her, after having initially sent positive signals to the customer who thus expected to be granted a loan. Being at the same time 'close to and competent for' customers created a problem if the advisor became too close to the customer and as a consequence lacked critical distance when offering loans. A quote reveals a similar dilemma for advisors hunting for new customers:

> We are requested to be aggressive in seeking new customers, but it is a problem when we have such strong internal regulations. You cannot phone a potentially new customer, get a positive response and then reject the customer because he does not suddenly satisfy the internal rules. (Advisor in interview)

However, the credit routine system and the distance between senior management and customers eased the pressure on advisors and office managers who did not have to make the unpopular decisions. As a consequence, this distance may cloud the senior management's knowledge of the advisors' customer competence, people skills, and detailed knowledge. To sum up, the advisors are clearly motivated by customer contacts and see these relationships as a potential for reflective learning, but this freedom for individual reflective practice is being confronted by stronger management control.

The bank's strategic learning initiatives

We now introduce the senior management's strategic learning initiatives and discuss how these initiatives manage and control employees' work. The four strategic and institutional learning initiatives for improved customer service are: 'Best Customer Practice'; information and accounting of learning activities; authorization; and training.

Best Customer Practice

The 'Best Customer Practice' is a manual about how advisors should prepare, conduct and review their customer meetings. In order to gain an overview of customer needs, meetings are planned in advance. The customer is then offered several products such as pension plans, savings targets, lifetime loans and insurance. From 2006 senior management required everybody in the bank to use this best customer practice with the aim of selling as many products as possible to each individual customer. The bank wants all advisors to complete two planned meetings with customers per day and record them in the balanced scorecard. The control initiative is then measured statistically in the scorecard and followed up by senior management.

In order to achieve these aims and organize time and information optimally, the bank wishes to change both advisor and customer habits. The advisors have to teach the customers to book an appointment. This turned out to be a difficult transition. One department, for example, put a wooden pallet in front of the advisors' offices with a large sign saying 'Remember to book an appointment at the counter'. On the very first morning, the first customer sneaked around the obstacle and barged into the advisor's office. The habits and demands for drop-in service both from customers and advisors are difficult to change. As a result, an advisor reported the need to discuss and reflect on how the advisors could use the best customer practice better:

> We should use more time on the work practices, how it is smart to work. We are too statistically controlled by using the balanced scorecard, instead of focusing on Best Customer Practice. It is annoying, but the senior management does not see this. (Advisor in interview)

As a part of the strategic plan, all new advisors have practised 'Best Customer Practice' in a three-month introduction course. Our data reveal that the practice is a useful tool for the majority of new advisors with no previous experience and no portfolio. New advisors implement 'Best Customer Practice' with greater ease than do experienced advisors. Nevertheless, experienced advisors are also using the 'Best Customer Practice' with positive outcomes:

> If you can be so structured then you have a great working day. I am very engaged in Best Customer Practice, I have used it and it has been a new world for me. (Advisor in interview)

These positive experiences are, however, seldom collectively reflected upon. In practice, the established routines of many experienced advisors connected to their large portfolios still influence many of their meetings with customers. By serving drop-in customers, as they always have been doing, the working day is fragmented and there is a lack of time and few opportunities for gathering information and preparing broad sales. When many of the experienced advisors are not following the process in practice, this means that the senior management's strategic initiatives are challenged:

> We do not take the time to implement new procedures. Best Customer Practice is a good example of a huge mistake. Even now at the end of 2009, still not everybody is using this tool. (Office manager in a meeting)

'Best Customer Practice' is particularly undermined in cases where experienced advisors continue as before, and sell more than the new advisors who loyally adhere to the new strategic plan. Their explanation is that sales of several products at the same time may paralyse the customer in making decisions to buy. Many advisors, therefore, based on their own experience, adopt a longer-term perspective in offering their products. In addition, a large and solid portfolio of regularly customers' erodes the time available to experienced advisors to use the 'Best Customer Practice'.

Information and accounting for learning activities

The analysis of the 2,284 recorded learning activities reveals that office management gave detailed information in 89% of the recorded activities. The information comprised four main topics: product presentations and manuals; summary of the balanced scorecard; sales and financial results; and new rules for processing loans (Antonsen, Thunberg, & Tiller, 2010). In reality, the learning activities appear to be about spreading performance operations determined by the organization and technology. The idea behind recording the activities was to increase the volume of learning and call attention to learning initiatives. Management and advisors see knowledge of products and regulations as an important basis for good customer contact. However, the strong focus on information and accountability cost the advisors much time to record their own progress in meeting objectives. One advisor described the increasing measuring in the scorecard as a problem:

> We don't think it should be necessary to use so much time on registering our activities. Senior management is designing measuring indicators without knowledge about advising, and advisors say it is not so easy to implement this frequent measuring in practice. (Advisor in interview)

The measuring had the side effect of lessening the focus on good quality customer service while increasing the emphasis on the quantity of sales activities that result in a bonus. Of all learning activitiesrecorded, 13% consist only of summaries of the results in the balanced scorecard. Our data about the presentations of the monthly balanced scorecard results in departments revealed that the numbers are usually reviewed with the comments 'this is good, satisfactory and here you have to improve'. The advisors did not participate in deciding the targets. As a consequence, information and the 'recording of registered learning' has been identified as 'learning', rather than actual improvements based on reflective learning. A focus group session discussed this topic and concluded that one-sided accounting and a too high a focus on presentations and products results in a problem for learning:

> Competence in relationships is not on the agenda when it comes to learning, and is not represented to the same extent as financial competence. It is competence in relationships which is our livelihood. (Office manager in focus group)

In the learning activities there is negligible registration of the intended focus areas of 'knowledge' and 'experience sharing'. There may, however, be under-registration of such learning as our interviews suggest that individual departments also focus on cooperation and sharing knowledge from experience, even though this has not been registered. Another explanation may be that among advisors, reflective learning from performing everyday tasks is hard to describe and therefore hard to measure. Because of the financial crisis of 2008, the bonus for registered learning was abandoned. The advisors started focusing less on accounting for learning activities and more on the new requirements for authorization.

Authorization

Advisors in Norwegian banks now have to gain a 'pass' and become authorized in order to keep their responsibilities. A theoretical and practical test must be passed. The theoretical content consists of personal economy, macroeconomics, financial markets, methods, portfolio composition, product groups, attitudes, ethics, the advisory practice, and rules and regulations. Testing of theoretical knowledge is completed via the Internet.

The financial business sector is behind this institutional qualification demand. The financial crisis made the initiative particularly relevant and accelerated its implementation, resulting in it becoming obligatory on 1 January 2009. All advisors must learn to ask obligatory ethical questions to make sure that the customer has understood which products he is buying, and thus prevent over-aggressive sales of so-called high-risk savings products such as hedge funds:

> One change is to reveal the needs of the customers. If the customer does not have a car, we should not sell him car insurance just to win a trip to Manchester! (Office manager in a meeting)

Our data reveal that the most experienced advisors have the greatest challenge in meeting the requirements, because they lack the theoretical basis for understanding the complex topic of macroeconomics. The theoretically educated, who have been selling high-risk saving products to the greatest extent, are best equipped for meeting the requirements. Of advisors in our case, 90% will never sell such products and are now spending much time during working hours and in their spare time studying for the authorization. Stress among the majority of advisors increased considerably when the two first advisors failed the practical test. This focus on individual authorization decreases time for reflective learning.

Training sessions

In order to pass the practical test to become authorized and increase sales in meetings with customers, the advisors need training sessions. These include training on the 'Best Customer Practice' that involves together practising simulated phone and face-to-face customer meetings in which important sales questions are posed to customers. Through role play as advisors, customers and observers, they regularly switch roles and practice techniques for increasing sales while using both their experiences and raising ethical questions. Here the advisors are assessed as 'pass' or 'fail' by a jury consisting of an office manager and an examiner employed by the bank. The fact that the practical authorization examination is conducted internally may strengthen the bank's control of and authority over the advisors.

All the advisors testify that such training methods create security and facilitate the sharing of experience:

> Sales training is practising customer meetings to become professional. This involves training to ask the important questions that makes you a good listener. (Advisor in meeting)

But some of our informants also point out that sales training that is limited to simplified cases may be problematic in developing long-term customer relations:

> If you push a product on the customer, you will not keep him for life. I wish to see an assertive drive in the behaviour of advisors. But there should not be a drive to sell life insurance. There should be a drive to get the customers to see for themselves what happens if they do not have life insurance. This is the inherent driving force. Your objective is to get the customers to understand their own needs. (Office manager in a meeting)

The informants say that there is not time for critical reflective learning before, during or after training sessions to improve sales and ethical questions. In dialogues between the advisors and the customers, the essential point is that the customers themselves can define their needs and wishes. The challenge is whether this can be promoted mainly through training routines or whether reflective learning is needed to improve the employees' competence and long-term customer relations (See Table 1).

The strategic learning initiatives constrains the opportunities for reflective learning

We argue that the idea of setting aside time for employees' learning is a good strategy, especially in financial organizations. However, our empirical findings indicate that advisors are faced by an overload of information and demands for accountability from senior management. The balanced scorecard's use of a 'Best Customer Practice' strategy, along with the authorization initiative and the training, are all designed to influence and control the objectives and the methods used by advisors in carrying out their responsibilities. Customer regard for the advisor and the building of trust are in danger of being choked by these new instrumental routines. Time for individual and collective reflective learning from customer relations is constrained by bank and institutional initiatives that emphasize control and security. The advisors' individual potential for reflective learning, influence and motivation decreases when work processes are turned into non-reflective routines and when both internal administrative and external documentation requirements are increased

Table 1. External constraints on team leader impact.

Performance process	Team-level constraints	Contextual constraints
Effort	Work inputs are under external control	Noble collective purposes
Performance strategy	Performance operations are organizationally or technologically determined	Strong institutional forces
Knowledge and skill	Work activities are simple and predictable	Skewed labour market

Source: Hackman and Wageman (2005).

to protect the customers' economic security. This finding is supported by a recent study confirming that employees are facing increased demands to keep their skills up-to-date, in parallel with attending to customer work (Goldman, Plack, Roche, Smith, & Catherine, 2009).

A top-down strategy that is too narrowly focused limits the opportunity for employees to contribute new ideas for change and development to improve the function and quality of work routines. Internal learning strategies combine with the external forces to constrain the employees' possibilities for reflective learning as summarized in Table 2.

The bank wishes to use the balanced scorecard and the 'Best Customer Practice' to streamline and standardize its products and services in order to achieve higher sales results. The vision of being 'close to and competent for' the customer in all customer relations creates possibilities for reflection on how learning can be more strongly derived from meetings with customers. The experienced advisors limit the amount of products they offer the customers in order to avoid decision-resistance by the customers. This quiet defiance of the 'Best Customer Practice' may help to explain the financial success of the bank. The tacit knowledge of the advisors derived from customer meetings seems to be underestimated in the overall learning strategy of the bank. This learning should contribute to making advisors' *close to and competent for* customers and high-quality meetings with customers also promote job satisfaction. Reflection among the employees about using the 'Best Customer Practice' could possibly develop and increase the use of the process in the organization. The balanced scorecard's focus on measuring, efficiency and tempo may have a constraining effect by using possible extra spare time on information and unreflective measurement and thereby pre-empting reflection. Such information does not develop the advisor–customer relationship and may damage the bank's competitive advantage in the long term. By reducing the amount of required information, employees may gain more time for reflective practice.

Highlighting only the visible overt actions in the balance scorecard means that tacit knowledge and reflective learning among employees are not recognized or valued in the development of the organization. In the balanced scorecard both invisible assets and reflective learning are difficult to measure and record. Another problem is that the data recorded will not identify frustrations or new possibilities for action that therefore cannot be followed up. As a consequence, such intangible factors are not communicated to the senior management, as also seen in Elg's (2009) study, and thus the potential for organizational learning is diminished (Argyris & Schön, 1996). Nevertheless, using the balanced scorecard does offer opportunities for employees to reflect on results and also on intangible factors with the intention of

Table 2. Constraints on reflective learning.

Performance process	Team-level constraints on reflective learning	Contextual constraints on reflective learning
Effort	The bank's ambition: 'close to and competent for' all customers	Customer demands
Performance strategy	Balanced scorecard 'Best customer practice'	Authorization credit routines
Knowledge and skill	Training product knowledge	

improving established practices and customer relations and of improving sales. The balanced scorecard has potential for increasing advisors' participation in organizational development if the senior management encourage and listen to such reflective practice.

The noble contextual demands of a bank to give customers financial support contains ethical challenges with which the advisor must cope. New authorization and credit routines aim to protect both banks and customers. The demands for internal control, regulations and information are increasing rapidly in financial organizations at the same time as they are challenged by owners and government to increase revenues. Senior management implements and controls the strategies. This creates a dilemma for advisors who are encouraged by senior management to increase the sales of products to customers at the same time as caring for the liquidity of the customers. Advisors simultaneously take the responsibility and the blame for handling customers and revised performance criteria. In other words, they are asked to use the accelerator and the brakes at the same time!

Conclusion

Reflective learning among employees is valued as essential for long-term development in organizations (Boud et al., 2006). However new management systems such as the balanced scorecard are introduced with the purpose of making organizations function more effectively using top-down control. We asked how the use of the balanced scorecard and new institutional demands influence the practice of reflective learning among advisors who provide customer service. Our findings show that the senior management's learning initiatives in fact are focused on organizational control rather than reflective learning. Advisors use their time to learn detailed product knowledge and work instructions, while senior managers organize this process. This contradicts the bank's written strategic plan for learning that advocates reflective learning for all advisors. The four strategic learning initiatives outlined above also contradict advisors' statements about how they learn customer service by means of reflective practice, a form of learning that they claim offers high value for the organization. Our findings show that rhetoric about reflective learning is not substantially realized in implementing the bank's learning strategies, despite the high value that advisors place on such learning as a means of improving their practice.

The bank's four strategic learning initiatives present advisors with dilemmas concerning sales and control work resulting from bank and external authorization requirements. As a result, the time available and the opportunities for individual and collective reflective learning are limited. The impact of the training, authorization and information lead advisors to become, in Schön's (2010) terminology, 'experts' rather than reflective practitioners. The learning initiatives offer the advisors few opportunities to participate in and influence policy-making, strategic planning, objective-setting and work tasks. The top-down learning strategies thus contradict current theories of workplace learning which emphasize development of employees through participation and empowerment. The strengthening of organizational control may not be the senior management's intention; however, a critical question is whether the learning initiatives become manipulative because they control activities (Illich, 1973). More research is needed about how the use of the balanced scorecard and top-down learning strategies emphasize control and decrease reflective learning. Our case study suggests that using advisors as scapegoats in the current financial crisis should be re-evaluated. Ideally, learning strategies that incorporate employees' reflective learning sufficiently to advance quality assurance may help prevent a new financial crisis.

References

Antonsen, Y., Thunberg, O.A., & Tiller, T. (2010). Adaptive learning and reduced cognitive uncertainty in a financial organization. *Journal of Workplace Learning, 22*(7), 475–488.

Argyris, C., & Schön, D.A. (1996). *Organizational learning II theory, method, and practice.* Reading, MA: Addison-Wesley.

Bazeley, P. (2007). *Qualitative data analysis with NVivo* (2nd ed.). London: Sage.

Boud, D., Cressey, P., & Docherty, P. (2006). *Productive reflection at work – learning for changing organizations.* London: Routledge.

Dewey, J. (1991). *How we think.* NY: Promethus Books.

Edmondson, A. (1999). Psychological safety and learning behavior in work teams. *Administrative Science Quarterly, 44*(2), 350–383.

Elg, M. (2009). Vilken betydelse har mätetal for ledarskapet i en teamorganiserad verksamhet? In P.-E. Ellström & H. Kock (Eds.), *Mot ett förändrat ledarskap?: om chefers arbete i team- och processorganiserad verksamhet* (pp. 105–126). Linköping: Studentlitteratur.

Ellström, P.-E. (2001). Integrating learning and work: conceptual issues ans critical conditions. *Human Resource Development Quarterly, 12*(4), 421–435.

Fenwick, T. (2008). Understanding relations of individual collective learning in work: A review of research. *Management Learning, 2008*(39), 227–243.

Flohr Nielsen, J., & Preuthun Pedersen, C. (2003). The consequences and limits of empowerment in financial services. *Scandinavian Journal of Management, 19,* 63–83.

Giddens, A. (1990). *The consequences of modernity.* Cambridge: Polity Press.

Glaser, B., & Strauss, A.L. (1967). *The discovery of grounded theory: Strategies for qualitative research.* Chicago, IL: Aldine.

Goldman, E., Plack, M., Roche, C., Smith, J., & Catherine, T. (2009). Learning in a chaotic environment. *Journal of Workplace Learning, 21*(7), 555–574.

Hackman, J.R., Wageman, R. (2005). When and how team leaders matter, In B. Staw & R. Kramer (Eds.), *Research in organizational behavior*, vol. 26 (pp. 36–74). San Diego, CA: Elsevier, JAI Press.

Hochschild, A.R. (2003). *The managed heart: Commercialization of human feeling* (20th anniversary ed.). Berkeley, CA: University of California Press.

Illich, I. (1973). *Tools for conviviality.* London: Calder & Boyars.

Jarvis, P., Halford, J., & Griffin, C. (2003). *The theory and practice of learning* (2nd ed.). London: Kogan Page.

Kaplan, R.S., & Norton, D.P. (1996). *The balanced scorecard: Translating strategy into action.* Boston, MA: Harvard Business School Press.

Krugman, P. (2009). How did economists get it so wrong? *New York Times,* 2 September.

Michel, A., & Wortham, S. (2009). *Bullish on uncertainty. How organizational cultures transform participants.* New York: Cambridge University Press.

Mintzberg, H., Ahlstrand, B., & Lampel, J. (1998). *Strategy safari – a guided tour through the wilds of strategic management.* New York: The Free Press.

Nilsen, E.A. (2007). *Oversettelsens mikroprosesser om å forstå møtet mellom en global idé og lokal praksis som dekontekstualisering, kontekstualisering og nettverksbygging.* Tromsø: Universitetet i Tromsø, Det samfunnsvitenskapelige fakultet.

Nonaka, I., & Takeuchi, H. (1995). *The knowledge-creating company: How Japanese companies create the dynamics of innovation.* New York: Oxford University Press.

Nørreklit, H. (2003). The BSC: What is the score? A rhetorical analysis of the BSC. *Acounting, Organizations and Society, 28,* 591–619.

Paranjape, B., Rossiter, M., & Pantano, V. (2006). Performance measurement systems: Successes, failures and future – a review. *Measuring Business Excellence, 10*(3), 4–14.

Radnor, Z.J., & Barnes, D. (2007). Historical analysis of performance measurement and management in operations management. *International Journal of Productivity and Performance Management, 56*(5/6), 384–396.

Røvik, K.A. (2007). *Trender og translasjoner ideer som former det 21. århundrets organisasjon*. Oslo: Universitetsforlaget.

Schön, D. (1987). *Educating the reflective practioner*. Ashgate, London: Jossey-Bass.

Senge, P.M. (1999). *The dance of change: The challenges of sustaining momentum in learning organizations*. New York: Currency/Doubleday.

Vince, R. (2002). Organizing reflection. *Management Learning, 2002*(33), 63–78.

Voelpel, S.C., Leibold, M., & Eckhoff, R.A. (2006). The tyranny of the BSC in the innovation economy. *Journal of Intellectual Capital, 7*(1), 43–60.

Wilkinson, S. (2004). Focus group research. In D. Silverman (Ed.), *Qualitative research: Theory, method and practice* (pp. 177–199). London: Sage.

Advancement of guided creative and critical reflection in the professional development of enterprising individuals in business and nursing

Ruth Anne Fraser[a] and Jasna K. Schwind[b]

[a]*Fraser Education, Uxbridge, ON, Canada;* [b]*Daphne Cockwell School of Nursing, Ryerson University, Toronto, ON, Canada*

Using narrative inquiry theoretical framework with creative and critical reflection to explore the personal and the professional lives of enterprising individuals reveals how metaphors, when used within the context of professional development in business and nursing, may open gates to expand and deepen reflective process and growth. Business and nursing individuals participate in guided creative and critical reflection on their lived experiences to recreate knowledge and understanding of themselves as workers in order to reconstruct their professional profiles for improved workplace discourse. The article explores the potential of guided creative narrative reflection and metaphor in the professional development of enterprising individuals in business and nursing.

Introduction

Although many employers from large and small firms seek out motivated and industrious individuals, the knowledge these individuals bring to the workplace may be undervalued. Even among well-educated and long-standing employees, this situation brings personal and professional hardship. Being undervalued may have an even deeper effect on employees whose skills limit their job mobility. Overcome by feelings of entrapment, these employees may fear losing their jobs or being ostracized if their discontent became known; so, they remain silent. Such attitudes and behaviours hamper the freedom needed to grow, personally and professionally. Likewise, these attitudes often widen the gap among the diverse levels of participation in the workplace, which may prohibit the flow of information and the effective use of knowledge. These situations do harm to both an enterprising firm and its individual workers.

Oftentimes, fellow workers and managers in the workplace are unaware of what workers know. An individual's abilities or talents that fall outside the formal job description may go unnoticed and remain untapped. In such an environment, workers begin to underutilize their own knowledge. When those in authority only pay lip service to worker development, this gap remains. In this type of setting, where can workers go to build the self-worth needed to be productive? What can leaders do to help close that gap? What can be done to cultivate worker knowledge? Would it help if workers became aware of the three-dimensional workplace of person, place and time (Clandinin & Connelly, 2000) in which they live? Throughout our research, we have kept these questions before us.

The professional development opportunities existing within most businesses are often viewed as inadequate and disappointing because they do not help the worker balance the personal and the professional dimensions of their lives. The rewards these enterprising individuals hope for in their workplace may be thwarted by situations such as mergers, downsizing, new technologies and frequent turnover of staff and systems. From our experiences, workers report how the values, which give meaning to their lives, are difficult to preserve in such tumultuous situations.

In our research, through guided creative and critical reflection, business workers and nurses are able to recognize the values and images by which they live and so reconstruct new meanings that contribute to their professional knowledge. With new knowledge come new discourses and a reshaping of the worker, the workplace and thus the world. Unless we understand how we obtain and apply our knowledge, we are vulnerable to problematic uncertainty. Narrative inquiry (Clandinin & Connelly, 2000) accepts uncertainties as a fundamental condition of living. At the same time, narrative inquiry provides a way to reflect, uncover and create new meanings so that the exploration of uncertainty can shape new professional knowledge, meaningful workplace landscape and workers' discourse. The use of metaphor is one mode of narrative reflection that allows exploration of lived experiences and its role in creating professional knowledge. In this paper, two researchers, Anne and Jasna, reflect on how they use metaphor in their respective disciplines, business and nursing, to guide enterprising individuals towards professional growth and development.

Following the review of the narrative inquiry framework (Clandinin & Connelly, 2000), business workers' professional development framework (Figure 2) (Fraser, 2005), narrative reflective process (NRP) (Schwind, 2008) and the role of metaphor in reflective practice, we present accounts of two Canadian enterprising individuals: Kelly, a small business consultant; and Sandra, a critical care nurse. We conclude the article by reflecting on possible implications of narrative inquiry for professional development within business and nursing practices.

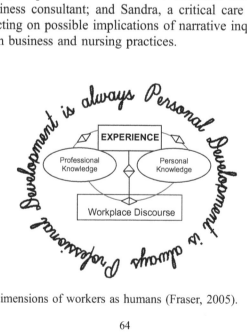

Figure 1. Holistic dimensions of workers as humans (Fraser, 2005).

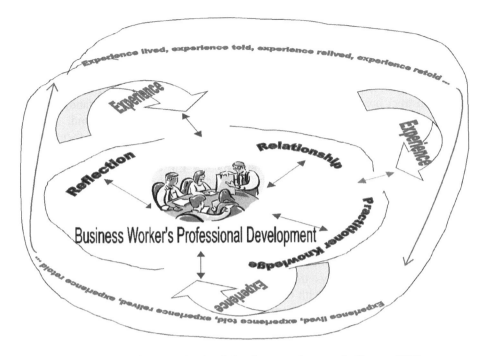

Figure 2. Business worker's professional development framework (Fraser, 2005).

Creative and critical reflection in the context of this article refers to reflective practices intended to incite change, and consequently the contexts in which enterprising individuals find themselves. Creative and critical reflection is important for professional development as persons become aware of their own histories and possible future alternatives. Through creative and critical reflection, professionals' lived metaphors may emerge, reveal their knowledge and enable transformative potential for growth and meaning to surface (see Figure 3).

Figure 3. Kelly's professional metaphor (Fraser, 2005).

Theoretical reflections

Narrative names the phenomenon and the manner in which it is studied. According to Carter (1993, p. 6), 'a narration is the symbolic presentation of a sequence of events connected by subject matter and related by time'. Through the reflective process of narrative inquiry that may include metaphor, we tell and re-tell, construct and re-construct our stories of experience in order to deepen understanding of our life events. In our work, we use narrative reflective process (Schwind, 2008) to engage enterprising individuals in personal self-awareness to help them further develop their professional practices.

As workers, our behaviour is coloured by our life experiences. These experiences form our 'attitudes that are emotional and intellectual, [covering] our basic sensitivities and ways of meeting and responding to all the conditions which we meet in living' (Dewey, 1938, p. 35). Our personal life narratives interweave with our professional stories to form a unity, which is our life. The personal experience component of this whole is defined by Connelly and Clandinin (1988, p. 59) as 'a moral, affective, and aesthetic way of knowing life's educational situations', which addresses the different ways that enterprising individuals' life experiences affect how they work and interact with one another.

Our research experiences are designed to lead participants to a deeper awareness of inquiry and the enterprising life they are living. In our respective research, we focus on the growth of individual workers who tell their stories, both personal and professional. Growth is a common dimension of narrative inquiry and professional development. Our research uses narrative to inquire about the ambiguity of personal practical knowledge (Clandinin, 1986) as our discourse in the workplace. We believe all enterprising individuals live their inquiry and are therefore working in a three-dimensional space (Clandinin & Connelly, 2000).

These thoughts bring us back to the importance of the three-dimensional narrative inquiry space described by Clandinin and Connelly (2000). Our application of this three-dimensional space to enterprising individuals in business and nursing is as follows: workers' practice can be described as personal and social, directed inward and outward, on a workplace landscape, in relationship with self and others, over a continuum of time (see Figure 4). In other words, a worker's context has a past, present and future, and the individual's place of practice encompasses the situations workers experience. As such, the situations enterprising individuals live have internal and external conditions that inform who they are as professionals (Dewey, 1938).

The key premise of narrative inquiry in the context of enterprising individuals is pictorially represented in Figure 1. In other words, who we are as persons is who we are as professionals (Connelly & Clandinin, 1999), meaning that the personal and the professional development of workers are intrinsically linked. Put another way, we bring all of our personal experiences into each and every one of our professional situations, and these experiences impact, whether we are aware of them or not, all of these encounters (Dewey, 1938).

Narrative accounts of our experiences bring them to life and therefore naturally involve reflection; this allows metaphors to come to light, making them available for discovery and exploration. As a result, in creative and critical reflection, unexpected meanings that lay buried in the experience may reveal that 'knowledge and skill in one situation [become] an instrument of understanding and dealing effectively with

Figure 4.   A tessolation: Anne's transformed professional image (Fraser, 2005).

the situations which follow' (Dewey, 1938, p. 44). Furthermore, through creative and critical reflection on lived experiences enterprising individuals' metaphors may emerge, deepening the narrative reflective process (Schwind, 2008) (see Figure 5).

Business worker's professional development conceptual framework

Our passionate interest in lived experiences as a way of knowing has made professional growth for business and nursing workers principal objectives for us. Through our respective inquiries, we create opportunities for workers to remodel their lived experiences, reconstruct knowledge, and professionally grow as enterprising individuals. This interest, which resulted from narrative inquiry into our personal experiences, led to our resolve to explore ways of helping workers achieve professional growth and satisfaction.

Figure 5.   Sandra's life metaphor (Schwind).

Every personal experience is in some way a social experience worthy of our reflection. Clandinin and Connelly (1996) believe that knowledge has the power to transform, and they have contributed a great deal to the advancement and support of inquiry into practitioner knowledge. Today, the world has fewer apparent geographic boundaries and enterprising entities play a central role in global development. At the same time, these enterprises rely on the knowledge of its workers that may be able to transcend limitations and nourish the world in which we live. Likewise, the work of nurses is pivotal to the health and well-being of those who are ill. Nurses are well positioned to apply their knowledge for the improvement of others. Clandinin and Connelly's (1996, p. 25) notion of professional knowledge landscapes 'composed of relationships among people, places and things ... as both an intellectual and a moral landscape' is a useful frame of reference to support our work.

The conceptual framework of business worker's professional development (Fraser, 2005), pictorially represented in Figure 2 revolves around the enterprising individual within a business context and narrative as a form of inquiry into experiences. In this interdisciplinary article, authors demonstrate how this business worker's professional development conceptual framework, which uses narrative as a way to inquire, is potentially transferable to the nursing context. Our respective undertakings use the process of reflection and relationship with others, leading to an increased understanding of practitioner knowledge. Each of these is placed within the general context of workers' lived and reconstructed experiences.

The social sciences study humans who live in relation with the world. Therefore, it is fundamental that our inquiry takes experience as its starting point. There is a large body of research to support the exploration of personal experiences as phenomena rich in meaning and knowledge that are relevant to our professional situations (Chan & Schwind, 2006; Chan, Cheung, Mok, Cheung, & Tong, 2006; Connelly & Clandinin, 1999; Dewey 1958; Fraser 2003; Lindsay & Smith, 2003; Maggisano, 2008; Morgan 1997; Schön 1983; Schwind 2003). Plato, for one, clearly affirms sense-experience as the 'source' of all our primary ideas: 'We are agreed also upon this, that we have not obtained this thought and could not have obtained it except by sight or touch or some other of the senses' (Khashaba, 2005, p. 75a).

For Dewey (1938, p. 48–49), 'the most important attitude that can be formed is the desire to go on learning, ... for when persons lose the desire to learn, they lose the ability to extract meaning from their experiences as they occur'. This idea is central to our research because, if workers lose the desire to learn, where can they look for meaning in their practice? How can they grow as enterprising individuals? The 'educative' (Dewey, 1938) nature of a professional development experience could itself maintain a worker's openness to learning. Since 'every experience influences, in some degree, the objective conditions under which further experiences are had' (Dewey, 1938, p. 37), it follows that the business pulse, to some extent, hinges on decision-making and growth. This situation is also evident with nurses upon whom health decisions often depend. It follows, then, that useful professional development of enterprising individuals can be invaluable. 'Seldom is a decision-demanding situation completely new, [as] it almost always contains one or more familiar elements' (Pollock, 1982, p. 40). Therefore, it is logical to propose that knowledge of how experiences may influence future objective conditions offers workers a distinct advantage. Narrative inquiry into experience upholds personal and professional growth.

Managerial and organizational practices are manifestations of its human values, beliefs, skills and desires (Fitz-enz, 1997). Therefore, it seems reasonable to assume that reflection-on-practice may promote deepened understanding of a small firm's principles of effectiveness. Dewey's (1933) philosophy influences our discussion of reflective practice for entrepreneurs; he defines reflective thought as 'active, persistent, and careful consideration of any belief or supposed form of knowledge in the light of the grounds that support it and the further conclusions to which it tends' (p. 118). Our inquiry into creative and critical reflection in the professional development of enterprising individuals makes no distinction between workers via workplace disciplines, management echelons, work experience, job descriptions, cultural or gender circumstances and performance issues that may be the focus of traditional development or coaching models (Flaherty, 1999, p. 121). We work from a narrative perspective that embodies temporality and always occurs between the personal and the social (Dewey, 1938, 1958, Clandinin & Connelly, 2000). Workers live lives: being a worker is a holistic experience. The personal and professional are inseparable. As such, workers seek meaning in their own way. Workers own and reconstruct knowledge using their experiences. Existing models influenced our inquiry; Schön's (1983) notion of 'reflection-in-action' (p. 49) is relevant because reflection is a critical dimension of knowledge-building for professionals. A fundamental distinction is that our inquiry goes beyond reflective practice as defined by Schön's (1983). In fact, our inquiry does not confine itself to reflection-on-practice, and 'in action' (Schön 1983, p. 50). Rather, we look beyond a worker's practice for reflective opportunities. Workers in our inquiry find knowledge in their lived experiences over time, in their cultural and family histories and within the places and relationships that shape them as workers. We posit that only when workers explore these facets of their lives can they articulate what they know. Narrative inquiry is the means and venue we selected to make this journey.

Likewise, Peter Drucker (2001) influences our inquiry. Drucker's contributions to models of volunteerism, leadership and values are of profound significance for workers. Referring to Drucker's (2001, p. 223) views, 'To be effective in an organization, one's own values must be compatible with the organization's values'. Our inquiry goes beyond the compilation of characteristics and narratives (Denning, 2005) an organization may use to describe its values. For us, as narrativists, this approach is incomplete. Our inquiry researches the business worker's and nurse's knowledge, modelled on Clandinin and Connelly's (1996) study of teachers' knowledge and current research about nurses' knowledge (Chan & Schwind, 2006; Lindsay, 2008a; Schwind, 2009). Our inquiry brings forth awareness that our participants embed into their professional insights and models reflective practice as iterative, forward moving and focussed on personal–professional interconnectedness, thus expanding future social impact. Best practice responses are lasting and apply in any business situation when they are fundamental to human interaction. Experience is central to human living. Oftentimes workers are entrenched in familiar roles. This leads to the expectation that what happens once will happen again. As humans, we develop patterns of mind and make meaning based upon the patterns we establish. In a work context, experience that shifts our perspectives may be transformative and expand workers' personal and professional knowledge (Cranton, 2006). Critical reflection encourages shifts in perspective, which may enhance the effectiveness of entrepreneurial decision-making.

Decision-making is for the future, and the future can only be reached through the present (Drucker, 1973). Here we see Drucker's ideas intersecting with those of Dewey (1938), who writes, 'we have the problem of ascertaining how acquaintance with the past may be translated into a potent instrumentality for dealing effectively with the future' (p. 23). If enterprises are going to develop in a healthy and wise way, we believe one of the principal roles for professional development will be to find strategies to make workers' knowledge productive and accessible. Inquiry into experience can offer profound contributions to our understanding of practitioner knowledge. Narrative inquiry into the worker's experience ultimately affects the enterprise and the enterprising individual.

Worker's images are integral to relived experiences, and pictorial representations offer insight and understanding about one's practice. Acknowledging corporate workers as enterprising in business, and nurses as enterprising in healthcare, we believe their respective personal experiences are the source of their knowledge and workplace discourse. We present professional development and education as interchangeable terms. For Dewey (1938), professional development (education), experience and life are threaded together, and therefore our inquiry into professional development of workers is an inquiry into their experience.

Metaphor is a potent literary device and supports inquiry. It stimulates imagination and may allow one person to understand another's perspective by the implications inherent in the suggested image. In the context of this paper, metaphor encourages readers to make their own connections with our viewpoints, enabling them to expand and extend their meanings. We have chosen to use metaphor in our research to encourage engaging responses. For many reasons, theatre is Anne's metaphor of choice as she imagines that 'all the workplace is a stage' for enterprising business individuals. Anne imagines workers on a workplace stage and reflects on the characters they describe in their stories. Jasna uses metaphor to help practicing nurses visualize and reconstruct meaning of the contexts within which they work and thereby become agents of change towards healthier futures.

Methods

Engaging workers in a creative and critical reflective process provides opportunities to expand their professional development where they gain appreciation of their personal and professional stories of experience and the metaphors they hold. Along with the explicit metaphors, implicit metaphors are embedded in everyday living. Lakoff and Johnson (2003) suggest that conceptual systems govern how people relate to their world within and without, and as such are central to how experience is understood. Such understanding and insight open new possibilities for more meaningful discourse within a work enterprise. Consciously or unconsciously, our life experiences shape our metaphors, and reciprocally we compose, reshape and recreate our living spaces using these metaphoric images. Thus, through metaphors, enterprising individuals are able to more fully explore and understand the significance of various life events that contribute to who they are as persons and professionals. The following two examples demonstrate Anne's work with Kelly and Jasna's work with Sandra:

Anne's work with Kelly

I was motivated to inquire into the professional development of workers because of relationships I had formed over the years among my university and continuing education students, my co-workers and my friends. Within these relationships, I observed how many enterprising individuals today appear to be rendered powerless by the fast pace and the changing conditions within their working environments. Through conversations and shared experiences, I heard workers' stories that often revealed deep dissatisfaction in their workplace.

I inquire openly into workers' personal and professional values, not as fixed principles written in stone, but as changing, growing and having origins fundamental to understanding knowledge. In order to support workers who pursue personal and professional growth, an integral part of my work is dedicated to helping individuals find ways to make Personal Practical Knowledge (Clandinin, 1986) both explicit and social, so it can contribute to successful and satisfying workplace practice. Through my ongoing inquiry, I created a 'professional development theme-based process' (Fraser, 2005), which workers can use to reconstruct, understand and apply their knowledge, in order to experience greater fulfilment within the professional landscape. I encourage stories from any period in workers' lives, but I always have one specific goal in mind: to have them bring to life a description of their professional profile in the workplace.

The themes I selected were ideas based on my own personal workplace customs and those suggested through discussion with my colleagues. This theme-based process invites workers to write stories about various topics. For example, I embark on the process with Kelly, a small business consultant, by asking her to narrate the following five themes in written story form. First, to describe an account of an experience with an authority figure in her life that has had an enduring effect on her. Second, to portray an imaginary 'bouquet of flowers' in which each flower represents an event or experience in her life. Third, to recall and discuss an art form such as a musical work, painting, theatre production, literary piece, poem, etc. that brings her back to an important event. Fourth, to write a letter of recognition to a co-worker she considers the 'best' colleague. The final narrative piece, which went beyond workplace narratives and wove together the intersecting patterns, represents Kelly's professional profile. She reflected on her themed stories, excerpts of which are presented here.

Kelly's experience with theme-based narrative inquiry

During my professional development inquiry with Kelly, she works out her professional profile, and writes the following rule in what she calls her 'manifestations of knowledge'.

> Everyone I work with, work for or who works for me gets treated the same; that is cordially, professionally and with dignity. We are souls with personalities, not personalities with souls. I attempt to discover or uncover everyone's 'gold nuggets'. I learn from these nuggets and use them to successfully accomplish work. (Field Notes: Kelly, June 2002)

Kelly's professional profile documentation resembled an academic assignment for a university course. She included a page with images, such as a gold miner and a spider web, to illustrate what she considered helpful portrayals of metaphors of her professional practice.

Kelly's description of herself as a professional, searching for 'gold nuggets', the talents of her clients and trainees, brought to mind her patience and awareness of detail as she sifts for meaning. Kelly concluded her professional paper with specific reflections about narrative inquiry and the ways it assisted her to understand and value her professional profile. Kelly refers to her professional attributes as practice in progress – her manifesto. She views communication as a conduit and valuable resource:

> Work goes more smoothly and successfully if the whole team recognizes each other as team members and is comfortable sharing skills and information. I keep in mind the same thing does not motivate everyone and add that to my list of goals for a project. (Professional Profile Notes: Kelly, 8 July 2002)

As I reflect on my inquiry experience with Kelly, I noticed that she would never give up trying to help someone learn. She treated her clients with personal respect, working beyond billable hours, often without their knowledge, in order to deliver an excellent product. Her narrative helps me to understand the regard Kelly holds for her colleagues and friends. Kelly's narrative is an example of the possibilities of unity between workers' personal and professional practices; our workplace discourse is rooted in our personal lived experiences. Workers can learn from Kelly's reflections; it is crucially important to know and believe in one's fundamental nature. Kelly's mindfulness of her own personal struggle to grow, to be authentic and to explore her potential, has empowered her to help others do the same.

Working with Kelly drew me into my own reflection on imagery and metaphor, and I became aware of new dimensions of myself as a researcher and a worker. A tessellation depicts the transformative stages of my professional image as it morphs from a blue spruce tree to a candle.

As I think about the change in my own professional image, I see how a new perspective can alter my landscape as well. My landscapes are not separate from me. If you change the worker, you change the workplace. This insight allowed me to think more deeply into Kelly's creative work. I also came to recognize that all enterprising workers who undergo transformation through critical reflection, *de facto* change the landscape within which they work. In other words, our images imbed our professional knowledge.

Jasna's work with Sandra

Today's healthcare agencies in North America are often viewed and managed as business enterprises. Although this fact is rarely made explicit to general public, its tenets are tangible because of how these healthcare systems view their workers and patients, who are often referred to as 'consumers of healthcare'. These enterprises may range in size from individual nursing care, to private nursing homes, to community and regional hospitals. Nurses who strive to provide holistic patient care within such professional landscapes require creative measures to sustain personal and professional growth and development.

My interest in healthcare focuses on the humanness of care within the therapeutic relationships (Schwind, 2008). To that end I have been working with nurses as they strive to enhance their caregiver roles within busy and highly demanding contexts. To gain a deeper understanding of nurses' life experiences as they endeavour to provide holistic patient care, I use different forms of narrative expression encapsulated in narrative reflective process (Schwind, 2008). This process grows out of narrative inquiry (Clandinin & Connelly, 2000) and encompasses such creative reflective tools as storytelling, creative writing, drawing and metaphor. Of the four creative tools, metaphor is often the one that brings forth unexpected epiphanies as the reflective process unfolds. Metaphors, when used as part of NRP, allow for increased self-awareness that may not have been evident earlier (Schwind, 2009) (see Figure 6). This unexpected 'aha' becomes a springboard for further reflective work with the opportunity for intentional growth and development.

Over the past while I have implemented NRP with patients, students and nurses. For the purposes of this article, I focus on my research experience with a set of enterprising individuals, busy nurses within a high stress environment. Facilitating their understanding of how they make sense of their own professional roles provides these workers with options for growth and development. Their self-awareness and knowledge play an integral role in how they interact with those in their care as well as with their peers. By engaging in creative and critical reflection, these enterprising individuals are exploring new boundaries so that they can make sense of and thereby contribute more effectively to the functioning, development and growth of the healthcare enterprise within which they work. To that end, I share one nurse's experience with the narrative reflective process, which includes the use of metaphor, to demonstrate how it can be implemented with healthcare workers. Nurse Sandra is a worker within a small community hospital critical care unit.

In my role as nurse-researcher, I decided to explore, using NRP, how critical care nurses conceptualize themselves as persons and professionals, who are also caregivers to patients experiencing traumatic events. I worked with several small groups of nurses. The process consisted of the following steps: sharing a 'safe' per-

Figure 6.   Sandra's caregiver metaphor (Schwind).

sonal story; choosing a life metaphor; drawing that metaphor; choosing a caregiver metaphor; looking at both metaphors and making connections between the personal and the professional; reflecting on how the two inform each other; and how this awareness could impact their respective professional roles (Schwind, 2008).

Sandra's experience with NRP

Sandra is a woman in her mid-thirties with a young family. She depicts her life metaphor as an octopus: 'a multi-tasker, multi-talented, with the ability to juggle ... its body being the center of all the parts that are being juggled'. In response to the question 'how are you like your metaphor?', Sandra shared: 'I am a multi-tasker, but I do forget to think about myself. Without looking after the center, the parts may not thrive'. When asked to consider how her metaphor helps her understand herself as a professional, after some thought Sandra concluded, 'If I am going all the time so selflessly I may not be able to sustain my ability to give'.

Sandra is a critical care nurse leader, who is responsible for supporting and guiding bedside nurses' professional growth. Sandra chose a coach and a cheer-leader as her caregiver metaphor. She sees herself as a 'coach who encourages and empowers her team; someone who guides novice colleagues and cheers them on ... a solid rock who can be depended upon'. Upon her reflection on the characteristics of her caregiver metaphor, Sandra writes: 'The metaphor helped me see myself as someone who truly cares about her [peers] and their success. I also see myself as assisting patients and advocating for them.'

In looking at the two metaphoric images, the personal and the professional, and how they intersect, Sandra summarized her notes: 'I am a multi-tasker who has a grounded centre with a soft side. I celebrate in the success of others.' With this self-awareness, Sandra considered how she could connect with her staff in a more meaningful way without compromising her own self-center and well-being. She also became cognizant of the high demands of both her personal and professional lives. She surmised that many of the critical care nurses were feeling similar demands on their energy level. As a result, she decided to role-model self-care practices for her colleagues, and thereby encourage them to engage in their own self-care activities.

Working with Sandra and her colleagues allowed me to reflect upon my own role as a teacher and how I live out my personal and professional metaphors. Not unlike Sandra, I recognized the selfless giving and care taking of those in my care. As I further reflected on this awareness, I was inspired by Sandra's resolve to role-model self-care and to set healthy personal and professional boundaries. In turn, I began to more intentionally encourage my students to do the same as they prepare for their future role as nurses within the highly demanding context of the healthcare enterprise.

Reflecting on my research experience with Sandra and her colleagues, narrative inquiry provided me with a framework that recognizes the role of personal experience within the professional landscape, and how a personal experience when creatively reflected upon has the power to impact the greater social environment. This work with nurses further demonstrates how the temporality and the quality of personal and professional lives mutually inform one another, and that 'who we are as persons is who we are as nurses' (Lindsay, 2008b, p. 19). Recognizing and valuing this relationship thus has significance for professional development and growth of enterprising individuals within workplace contexts.

Authors' reflections

In our participants' narratives, we heard their storied versions of their personal practical knowledge (Clandinin, 1986) as a way of understanding and improving their professional practice. Through narrative inquiry, the reflection on stories of experience includes creating useful knowledge for the advancement of enterprising practice. A major contribution of our respective inquiries is the voice it generates for those who act on the business and nursing stages. Throughout our individual research endeavours, participants' stories contributed workers' viewpoints about issues such as worker recognition, mentoring, balancing work and family, and living by certain values and principles. We believe the stories and experiences of our participants may influence and support other enterprising workers seeking professional growth and satisfaction. Resonance among workers' stories emphasizes the importance of sharing these accounts of experience and provides evidence that may be useful knowledge with far-reaching potential. Enhanced personal and professional knowledge becomes accessible when workers' lives resonate with one another. Reverberations that occur because of shared reflections may then prompt other individuals to recognize knowledge in their own stories. By reflecting on their stories enterprising individuals may come to terms with the knowledge and the images by which they consciously or unconsciously live. Workers may deepen their understanding of themselves and their workplace environments and the social dimensions in which they participate. The experience of personal value, social belonging and the connections among the individuals on the workplace stage may break barriers only penetrable by genuine human understanding. Workers' contributions may thus deepen experiences of humanness for other workers. Our discussion links worker stories of experience and critical reflection with the impact of personal values, responsibilities, commitments and recognition.

As we grapple with the development of reflective entrepreneurs, Schön enlightens us with his notion of the:

> practitioner who ... allows himself to experience surprise, puzzlement, or confusion in a situation which he finds uncertain or unique. He reflects on the phenomena before him, and on the prior understandings which have been implicit in his behaviour. (Schön, 1983, p. 69)

For a reflective professional, the similarities between situations allow knowledge to carry over creating an interface between past and present experiences. There is no separation between what we know and what we do. What we know from experience allows us to reframe the present situation. This may lead to a new understanding of the phenomena and support advantageous change. In this way, inquiry is built-in to the reflective professional's *modus operandi*. Workers who apply the insights and understandings they have acquired through creative and critical reflection tend to be more satisfied in their workplace because of the grasp they have on their situations. Consequently, satisfied workers may create unprecedented appreciation for others on the global stage.

In this creative and critical reflective process, images and metaphors emerge as a way for people to make sense of their experiences. Through awareness of their metaphors, enterprising workers shape their practice. Metaphoric images appear 'to link thinking with feeling, [hence bridging] the gap between the cognitive and affective domains' (Duit, 1991, p. 653). Bridging this gap empowers enterprising individuals to advance their practice and workplace satisfaction.

Implications for the field

Not only do images describe ourselves, but they influence us, too. When we describe our professional workplace selves, a metaphor can be a helpful tool. Our metaphors summon images that serve to influence our actions. The images we replay over and over in our mind's eye tell us about how we perceive our world, how we think and how we act, and, important for our research, how we are in our professional practice. One place to find our metaphors is in our stories of our experiences. Our stories tell us about how we see situations we have lived. Workers' stories can be relived and retold. Deeper reflection on their metaphors can change their professional practice and thereby their workplace landscape. Metaphors not only create knowledge for us but also represent our knowledge. The characteristics of our images are multi-dimensional, having a depth and intensity, which energetically portray what we are trying to understand.

Bateson (1989) talks about people's efforts to compose a life for themselves, how we all draw from many sources in the process. She offers powerful insight into the connections between the elements of our life; our very living is being in connections of all kinds: connected with others in relationships; connected with time, place and history; connected with change. In her words:

> Just as change stimulates us to look for more abstract constancies, so the individual effort to compose a life, framed by birth and death and carefully pieced together from disparate elements, becomes a statement on the unity of living. These works of art, still incomplete, are parables in process, the living metaphors with which we describe the world. (Bateson, 1989, p. 18)

The metaphors that come to light through guided creative and critical reflection have significant potential for effective professional development of enterprising individuals. As we have seen from our two examples, professionals may carry over their play scripts between home and work, between their personal and professional lived experiences. Persons reshape their professional landscapes. Thus, 'improvement' of professionals and their landscapes occurs simultaneously.

Professionals contribute on the world stage. Using Shakespeare's words 'All the world's a stage' (Shakespeare, 1976) assists us as we consider what is significant about narrative inquiry. How do professional play scripts make a difference in all the other dramas in the world? This is a central question for us. We are all actors on the same world stage and what we do within our enterprises, no matter how small, affects other performers and the stage itself. By using narrative as a form of inquiry, professionals, especially, are in a position to make profound and lasting contributions to multiple world stages, beyond their own specific disciplines, like business and nursing.

> Narrative inquiry has potential for understanding and shaping workplace communities and culture because it conveys profound and complex meaning for individual workers. Life-long learning rooted in the practice of inquiry may set knowledge creation in motion when workers experience understanding, meaning and even improved satisfaction in their workplace community. (Fraser, 2007, p. 2)

Narrative reflection enables worker's continuums to interweave, interconnect, and thus create new meaning for the present. Narrative binds the experiences of our lives. Through relationships, our narrative is recreated and relived in a new and present context. Without relationship in narrative, there is no new context, no back and forth, no inward outward, no place. Anne's 'theme-based professional development process' (Fraser 2005) and Jasna's 'narrative reflective process' (Schwind 2003) offer the possibility of new actions, new motives and new experiences; thus, new relationships, metaphors and professional re-creations of small firms and enterprising individuals. If we are open to reconstruction of our personal–professional selves through metaphors, then we create possibilities for the reconfiguration of our inter-disciplinary landscapes.

In this article, we have woven together the stories of our research experiences that used creative narrative reflection to explore enterprising individuals' metaphors, thus enriching their professional roles within the workplace context and beyond.

Narrative inquiry as reflective research has implications for how humans know, live and understand their lives in relationships, leadership and inter-disciplinary workplace practices. Reconstructing stories through narrative inquiry brings metaphors to light and can provide transformative influence at all levels of the professional landscape. Our respective research brings interprofessionalism within the professional contexts of business and nursing respectively. We are all in the same interdisciplinary 'basket' weaving global interdisciplinary narratives. A revised world story is possible as professionals deepen their mutual understandings through metaphors rooted in their narratives. Personal and professional metaphors provide a significant way for professionals to understand, co-construct and expand their worldview, and in this way find meaning in their work that reaches far beyond their individual needs.

Concluding remarks

Today, enterprising workers face many challenges, not the least of which is how rapidly change occurs. So much of daily workplace activity hinges on information-gathering and sharing. Incredible amounts of information are collected and made available through technological devices based upon computing and telecommunications. There is no telling what changes will emerge tomorrow and what new tools will be required in order to process information. Consider, then, the usefulness of personal storytelling as a form of inquiry into workplace knowledge. Information and knowledge may seem closely related, and, to some, even synonymous. In the context of this study, we see information as an ever-changing entity. Personal practical knowledge, on the other hand, has durability about it. This is not to imply that knowledge does not change. In many ways, knowledge does change. The process of reflection enables the reconstruction and creation of knowledge. Therefore, as we see it, changes in knowledge lead to growth, to something more than what came before. Growth occurs because of newfound meanings. However, it is important not to reduce our experiences to a single meaning. In her work, *Peripheral Visions*, Bateson beautifully states the idea of 'paths of insight':

> Sometimes a narrative, which seems to fit into one category metamorphoses into another. These are all ways of learning, by encountering and comparing more than one version of experience, that the realities of self and world are relative, dependent on context and point of view. (Bateson, 1994, p. 12)

Every moment we live is a new place in time. The experience of each moment is new and somehow different from those in our past. In this joint article, we have described two guided creative and critical reflection processes that support the possible evolution of new knowledge that lies dormant within our life experiences. New dimensions of knowledge are the underpinnings of new connections, new images, new contexts, new relationships and new meanings. Because our research is rooted in human experience, it is possible that evolving dimensions of knowledge experienced by business and nursing workers may be transferable to the professional development of other enterprising individuals.

Acknowledgement

This work was supported by the Travel Grant, awarded to J.K. Schwind, May 2010, by the Faculty of Community Services, Ryerson University, Toronto, Canada.

References

Bateson, M.C. (1989). *Composing a life*. New York: Grove.

Bateson, M.C. (1994). *Peripheral visions: Learning along the way*. New York: Harper Collins.

Carter, K. (1993). The place of story in the study of teaching and teacher education. *Educational Researcher, 22*(1), 5–12.

Chan, E.A., Cheung, K., Mok, E., Cheung, S., & Tong, E. (2006). A narrative inquiry into Hong Kong Chinese adults' concepts of health through their cultural stories. *International Journal of Nursing Studies, 43*, 301–309.

Chan, E.A., & Schwind, J.K. (2006). Two nurse-teachers reflect on acquiring their nursing identity. *Reflective Practice, 7*(4), 303–314.

Clandinin, D.J. (1986). *Classroom practice: Teacher images in action*. Philadelphia, PA: The Falmer Press, Taylor & Francis.

Clandinin, D.J., & Connelly, F.M. (1996). Teachers' professional knowledge landscapes: Teacher stories – stories of teachers – school stories – stories of schools. *Educational Research, 25*(3), 24–30.

Clandinin, D.J., & Connelly, F.M. (2000). *Narrative inquiry: Experience and story in qualitative research*. San Francisco, CA: Jossey-Bass.

Connelly, F.M., & Clandinin, D.J. (1988). *Teachers as curriculum planners*. Toronto: Teachers College Press.

Connelly, F.M., & Clandinin, D.J. (Eds.). (1999). *Shaping a professional identity: Stories of educational practice*. New York: Teachers College Press.

Cranton, P. (2006). *Understanding and promoting transformative learning: A guide for educators of adults*. San Francisco, CA: John Wiley & Sons.

Denning, S. (2005). *The leader's guide to storytelling: Mastering the art and discipline of business narrative*. San Francisco, CA: Jossey-Bass.

Dewey, J. (1933). *How we think*. New York: D.C. Heath.

Dewey, J. (1938). *Experience and education*. New York: Collier.

Dewey, J. (1958). *Experience and nature*. New York: Dover.

Drucker, P.F. (1973). *Management, tasks, responsibilities, practices*. New York: Harper & Row.

Drucker, P.F. (2001). *The essential Drucker*. New York: HarperCollins.

Duit, R. (1991). On the role of analogies and metaphors in learning science. *Science Education, 75*(6), 649–672.

Fitz-enz, J. (1997). *The 8 practices of exceptional companies: How great organizations make the most of their human assets*. New York: Amacom, American Management Association.

Flaherty, J. (1999). *Coaching: Evoking excellence in others*. Burlington, MA: Elsevier.

Fraser, R.A.K. (2003). *Narrative inquiry into personal practical knowledge in the workplace*. Paper presented at the Holistic learning: Breaking new ground, Toronto, Canada, October.

Fraser, R.A.K. (2005). *All the workplace is a stage – work as discourse: A narrative inquiry into workers' professional development* (Unpublished doctoral dissertation). Ontario Institute for Studies in Education of the University of Toronto.

Fraser, R.A.K. (2007). *Narrative inquiry: A research method and process enabling life-long learning influencing workplace communities and cultures.* Paper presented at the Standing Conference on University Teaching & Research for the Education of Adults. Belfast, Northern Ireland.

Khashaba, D.R. (2005). *Plato: An interpretation.* College Station, TX: Virtualbookworm. com Publishing.

Lakoff, G., & Johnson. M. (2003[1980]). *Metaphors we live by.* Chicago, IL: The University of Chicago Press.

Lindsay, G.M. (2008a). Thinking narratively: Artificial persons in nursing and healthcare. *Nurse Education Today, 28*(3), 348–353.

Lindsay, G.M. (2008b). Who you are as a person is who you are as a nurse: Construction of identity and knowledge. In J.K. Schwind & G.M. Lindsay (Eds.), *From experience to relationships: Reconstructing ourselves in education and healthcare* (pp. 19–36). Charlotte, NC: Information Age Publishing, Inc.

Lindsay, G.M., & Smith, F. (2003). Narrative inquiry in a nursing practicum. *Nursing Inquiry, 10,* 121–129.

Maggisano, C. (2008). Crafting an identity: Toward an understanding of the importance of self-definition in educational contexts. In J.K. Schwind & G.M. Lindsay (Eds.), *From experience to relationships: Reconstructing ourselves in education and healthcare* (pp. 1–15). Charlotte, NC: Information Age Publishing, Inc.

Morgan, G. (1997). *Images of organization.* Newbury Park, CA: Sage.

Pollock, T. (1982). *Managing creatively.* Boston, MA: CBI.

Schön, D. (1983). *The reflective practitioner: How professionals think in action.* New York: Basic Books.

Schwind, J.K. (2003). Reflective process in the study of illness stories as experienced by three nurse-teachers. *Reflective Practice, 4*(1), 19–32.

Schwind, J.K. (2008). Accessing humanness: From experience to research, from classroom to praxis. In J.K. Schwind & G.M. Lindsay (Eds.), *From experience to relationships: Reconstructing ourselves in education and healthcare* (pp. 77–94). Charlotte, NC: Information Age Publishing, Inc.

Schwind, J.K. (2009). Metaphor-reflection in my healthcare experience. *Aporia, 1*(1), 15–21. Retrieved from http://www.aporiajournal.com.

Shakespeare, W. (1976). *The complete works of William Shakespeare* (17th ed.). New York: Spring Books.

Reflective Learning and Clerical staff at a University College in the Cayman Islands: Implications for Management (An Exploratory Study)

Mark A. Minott, Allan E. Young and Carolyn Mathews

University College of the Cayman Islands

Whilst the concept of reflective learning has been extensively studied in the classroom, its role in business settings has not been the subject of significant research. This paper presents the outcomes of a small research study which focused on reflective learning and its application in a small organization. The main aim of the research was to ascertain the extent to which clerical workers were engaged in reflective learning while on the job and to outline the implications of this occurrence for small business management. A modified version of Valli's reflective typology was used to guide the research and to aid in achieving the aim. The main research instrument was a comprehensive questionnaire. The findings indicate that clerical staff at the University College predominantly engaged in reflection-on-action, reflection-in-action and personalistic reflective learning on the job. The implications of this occurrence for workplace learning, management and greater organizational efficiencies are discussed.

Introduction and outline

While there is an abundance of literature on reflective learning (RL) (Schon, 1983, 1987; Valli, 1997; Zeichner & Liston, 1996; Ghaye & Ghaye, 1999; Spaulding & Wilson, 2002; Minott, 2009, 2010a), the concept has been confined to the classroom. There are few studies which apply this teaching/learning methodology to business. This is so because a search of the terms, 'reflective learning' and 'business', or 'administration' on the Elton B. Stephens Company (EBSCO) data base returned two relevant articles (De Dea Roglio & Light, 2009; Munro & Cook, 2008). The British Education Index (BEI) free collection returned no articles and the Education Resources Information Center (ERIC) returned one article (Oliver, 2006). Given these facts, the aim of this investigation is threefold. Firstly, to aid in redressing the lack of attention given to the relationship between reflective learning and business. Secondly, and even more importantly, to investigate the extent to which clerical staff in a university college engages with RL while on the job. Thirdly, to discuss the implications of the findings and their application for management. To aid us in achieving this threefold aim and to guide the investigation, we used a modified version of Valli's (1997) typology of reflection.

We commence this paper with an outline of Valli's typology, a definition of RL and a discussion of potential indicators of clerical staff's use of RL on the job. We end with an outline of the study which forms the basis of the paper and a discussion of the implications of the findings for management.

Valli typology of reflection

A review of literature and a number of teacher education programmes, led Valli (1997) to conclude that there were six types of reflection utilized in teaching and learning: technical reflection; reflection-in-action and reflection-on-action; deliberative reflection; personalistic reflection; and critical reflection. In defining these types of reflection, Valli focused on the content for reflection and the quality of reflection. Content for reflection refers to what teachers thought about, and quality of reflection refers to how they thought about their teaching or the processes of thinking they go through. Valli (1997) explains each type of reflection and these are outlined here.

Technical reflective learning involves thinking about general instruction, that is, the teaching of techniques or skills. Teachers engaged in this type of reflection are directed by a straightforward application of research to teaching. They were also inclined to match their own performance to external guidelines established by education authorities and researchers. Reflection-in-action and reflection-on-action involves thinking about one's personal teaching performance or unique situation. This process also includes using one's values, beliefs, classroom context and students as sources of knowledge for action. Teachers engaged in this type of reflection made and justified decisions based on their unique situation and experience.

Deliberative reflective learning involves thinking about a whole range of teaching concerns, including students, the curriculum, instructional strategies and the rules and organization of the classroom. This type of reflection emphasizes decision-making based on teachers' personal beliefs, values, research, experience and the advice of other teachers. Teachers engaged in this type of reflection weighed competing viewpoints and research findings, and were able to give good reasons for the decisions they made.

Personalistic reflective learning involves thinking about one's own personal growth, relationships with students and improving students holistically. Teachers engaged in this type of reflection empathized with students and were very concerned with their affective needs.

Critical reflective learning involves thinking about the social, moral and political dimensions of schooling. The aim is to understand and improve the quality of life of disadvantaged groups. Teachers engaged in this type of reflection applied ethical criteria, such as social justice and equality of opportunity to the goals and processes of schooling.

Valli's typology has been criticized by Hatton and Smith (1995) as being hierarchical in nature. They state that reflection-in-action and reflection-on-action are the most complex and demanding of the five types of reflection, yet Valli placed critical reflection higher and seems not to have recognized this fact. They also argue that the end-point in the process of developing reflective practitioners is to develop their capacity to undertake reflection-in-action, which they consider to be the most demanding type of reflecting on one's own practice. In defence of Valli, Spaulding and Wilson (2002) point out that her typology of reflection is not hierarchical, and so one should not be tempted to value some forms of reflection more than others.

Despite these criticisms (and as indicated in the foregoing discussion), a modified version of Valli's typology was used to aid in the process of categorizing and determining the types of reflective learning in which clerical staff at a university college engaged. There were three reasons for selecting and implementing Valli's typology. Firstly, it was compiled after careful analysis of the works of many writers and in particular Donald Schon, who is revered as an architect in the development of reflective teaching and thinking. Schon (1987) argues for, and demonstrates the benefits of, reflection. He forwarded the idea that reflection occurred before, after, and during action. These he referred to as reflection-on-action and reflection-in-action. These and other ideas seem to undergird the construction of Valli's typology. Secondly, the typology is 'user friendly' and easy to follow. This is important, because it provided a template that standardized how reflective learning among clerical staff could be assessed. Thirdly, and most importantly, there was the need for a 'tool' to aid us in analysing staff reflective learning, and her typology of reflection enabled the process of analysis.

Reflective learning (RL)

Ghaye and Ghaye (1999) see reflection as thinking about what you do, and Farrell (2001) sees it as thinking critically about what you do, which involves recall, consideration and evaluation of experiences. For the purpose of our study, reflection is careful consideration or thought; it is a process of disciplined intellectual criticism combining research; knowledge of context, and balanced judgment (critical thinking) about previous, present, and future actions, events or decisions (Minott, 2009). Reflection does not exist in an abstract sense, but is enacted through job related tasks, actions, events or decisions. A common feature of the reflective learning process is the questioning of 'self', that is, one's belief, values, assumptions, context and goals, in relation to tasks, actions, events or decisions (Zeichner & Liston, 1996).

In light of this, reflective learning is an approach to problem-solving that uses reflection as the main tool. It encourages the individual to create distance between themselves and their practice. It also involves them analysing, discussing, evaluating, changing and developing their workplace practices, by adopting an analytical approach to their work. Sometimes this process is triggered by an experience or unexpected incident (Boyd & Fales, 1983). Brockbank and McGill (2007) agree with this definition when they state that reflective learning is a process that occurs in a social setting and it involves a context (workplace) and experiences (work-related tasks, events or situations). Individuals are actively engaged in the process and with others in open dialogue, with the expressed aim of transforming and improving self and the environment. So, to summarize, reflective learning is the use of critical thinking to aid in analysing, discussing and evaluating experiences so as to develop work-related knowledge and improve work-related practices. The process may also result in the discovery of new insights, theories and perspectives.

As indicated in this definition, critical thinking is a co-requisite of reflective learning.

It is characterized differently by various writers. Fowler (1996) lists over 15 definitions of critical thinking proposed by 15 different writers. There are some similarities as well as differences to these. An examination of the definitions suggests that the writers all agree on the fact that its binding characteristic is that it is primarily a mental or cognitive process with particular outcomes such as arriving at appropriate:

- beliefs;
- patterns of reasoning;
- conclusion of whether to reject or suspend judgment on an issue;
- understanding and meaning of an issue or statement;
- logical inferences;
- evidence and following where it leads; and
- decisions about material by distinguishing between facts and opinion.

This list of outcomes of critical thinking displays the different uses and results of the application of this cognitive skill. For example, critical thinking can be applied to a particular situation and a conclusion drawn with regard to what to believe or what actions to take, or it can result in making logical inferences. Having said that, what are potential indicators of clerical staff's use of RL on the job? It is to this question that we now turn our attention.

Reflective learning and clerical staff

To provide potential answers to the question above, we incorporate Villi's typology of RL in the discussion in this section.

Clerical staff duties

While the term clerical is traditionally associated with the clergy, it is also used in relation to office staff. It is this definition which guides our thinking. In any enterprise there are various types of clerical staff, for example, receiving clerk and/or order clerk who are responsible for receiving, stocking and billing, general office clerk, file clerk, mail clerk, payroll clerk, personal clerk and procurement clerk. In finance and banking, clerical staff includes: tellers; loan clerks; credit clerks; claims clerks; and many others (Degree Directory, 2010).

Traditionally, clerical work involves entry-level secretarial and administrative support positions and often includes answering phone calls and distributing mail, sorting and filing mail that no longer needs responses, making travel arrangement for managers, updating customers' records, typing of letters, briefs, reports and memos, copying and collating, record keeping, appointment scheduling, data entry, minor bookkeeping and low-level public relations. Other duties may include preparing envelopes, making signs, creating labels, ordering supplies, keeping track of inventory, running errands and setting up rooms for various meetings or helping people set up Powerpoint presentations (Pennypacker, 2009; Degree Directory, 2010).

These traditional duties of clerical staff are changing and to some extent have changed. Cummings (2009) points out that clerical staff are being given more responsibilities in the workplace and are called upon to manage projects. He argues that given the changing nature of the workplace, staff with excellent interpersonal skills and the ability to interact socially with customers, peers and management and who are able to build deeper work-related knowledge and develop technical skills will be more successful than those who rely on traditional clerical skills.

The introduction of technology has also revolutionized the functions of clerical staff. Today, their duties include the entry of data using spreadsheet software, the use of sophisticated computer systems, printers and copiers, and they need to be familiar with the software appropriate to their jobs and even how to maintain this software. Cummings (2009) also made the point that adaptive technology such as speech recognition, cell-phone cameras and various data systems pose a threat to jobs which only focus on routine clerical tasks, for example, typing, data entry and filing.

Clerical duties today are many and varied, says Pennypacker (2009); a duty such as answering the phone and taking messages now involves operating a complicated switchboard. In addition to answering the phone and taking messages and receiving packages, Smith (2010) points out that a clerical worker may also greet visitors, find out who they are, the employee they are there to visit, and inform the employee that they have a guest. This may also include directing the visitor to a waiting area and offering them a beverage. This is in line with the thoughts of Cummings (2009) that, increasingly, interpersonal skills are becoming more important for clerical workers to develop or cultivate.

As indicated in the forgoing discussion, clerical staff often make copies of documents on a photocopier or a printer and send documents via fax machine or regular mail. These duties may also include operating and maintaining such office equipment. This may include ensuring that copiers, fax machines and printers are running correctly and are supplied with paper. Attending to machinery breakdowns, by determining the problem and correcting it or contacting others to make repairs, are also duties of some clerical staff (Smith, 2010). These additional duties now demand that staff possess certain technical skills (Cummings, 2009). Another duty of the clerical staff worker is handling recycling bins, for example, being the point person for the recycling company that services the office and the shredding of confidential documents that should not be placed in the regular or recycle bin (Smith, 2010). An examination of these duties of clerical staff points to the need for them to be able to think in order to successfully carry out these duties. However, if they are to utilize RL on the job to develop work-related knowledge and improve workplace practices, they will need to be able to not just think, but to think critically.

Given the particular duties of clerical staff indicated above, their use of technical reflective learning on the job would involve critically thinking about the techniques and skills they utilize in order to carry out their varied duties. They would also critically think about their own personal performance or unique work situation and are directed by the need to apply personal theories to work-related matters. There would be an inclination to match their own performance to guidelines established by others in authority, and make and justify decisions based on their unique situation and experience. Their use of reflection-on-action on the job would include critically thinking about events or situations either before or after they have occurred, whereas reflection-in-action would include critically thinking – on the spot, in 'the thick of things', as discussed by (Schon, 1983) – about a job task or an event in which they are involved, sometimes having to assess, revise and implement new approaches and activities immediately. Adler (1994) states that critical to reflection-in-action is the ability to recognize problematic issues and to frame the context in which to attend to them. According to Schon (1987), framing means a staff member encountering an unexpected occurrence or situation selects – in a qualified and circumscribed sense – what will be treated as the problem, set the boundaries of his/ her attention to it, impose on it a coherence, which allows him/her to say what is wrong and in what direction the situation needs to be changed.

Smith (2001) makes the point that there is a clear relationship between reflection-in-action and reflection-on-action, because people draw upon the processes, experiences and understandings generated through reflection-on-action during reflection-in-action. While the ability to reflect in and on action is a means of dealing with situations of uncertainties, value conflicts and instability that may arise in the workplace, there are limitations to employing these actions while on the job. Van Manen (1995) states that given the immediacy and quick-changing nature of many work situations, it is not possible to use reflection-in-action in the fullest sense; in such situations, reflection in-action is only limited and restricted to the tasks at hand and cannot accommodate the full range of possibilities of interpreting what is going on, understanding and considering alternative courses of action, weighting their various consequences, deciding on what must be done and then actually doing it.

The important point to note is that in everyday workplace situations reflection-in-action is only possible in a qualified and circumscribed sense. Nevertheless, reflection-in-action does occur in a circumscribed sense. This also means that the thinking and subsequent action taken will be task- or situation-specific.

Clerical staff's use of deliberative reflective learning on the job would include critically thinking about a whole range of concerns, for example, their colleagues, the mission of the organization, the planning strategies being employed and the rules of the organization. They would make decisions based on personal beliefs, values, personal experiences and the advice of fellow staff members. Clerical workers engaged in deliberative reflective learning also weigh competing viewpoints and are able to give good reasons for the decisions they make.

Clerical staff utilizing personalistic reflective learning on the job would think critically about their own personal growth and relationships with colleagues. They empathize with others and would be very concerned with the affective needs of others. Their use of critical reflective learning on the job would involve thinking critically about the social, moral and political dimensions of the workplace. The aim would be to understand and improve the quality of life of those disadvantaged. They would apply ethical criteria, such as social justice and equality of opportunity for all in the workplace.

While the foregoing literature review highlights potential indicators of clerical staff's use of reflective learning in the development of knowledge and to improve workplace practice, what is still unknown is the extent to which clerical staff at the university college utilize RL in its various forms. Based on this question, a study was launched.

Method

As indicated in the foregoing discussion, the aim of the study was threefold. Firstly, to aid in redressing the lack of attention given to the relationship between reflective learning and business; secondly, and more importantly, to investigate the extent to which clerical staff in a local university college engages with RL while on the job; and thirdly, to discuss the implications of the findings for management. One broad research question guided the study: to what extent do clerical staff at a local university college engage with RL while on the job? In order to address the aims and respond to the broad research question posed, a mixed-mode methodology was employed. This involved the use of a comprehensive questionnaire and follow-up sessions.

Questionnaire and follow-up sessions

The questionnaire addressed the six categories of reflective learning espoused by Valli (1997): technical reflective learning; reflection-in-action; reflection-on-action; deliberative reflective learning; personalistic reflective learning; and critical reflective learning.

Questionnaires were numbered and individual participants were assigned a number which was only known to the researchers. The questionnaire also contained 30 Likert-type questions that measured the range of actions, feelings or perceptions regarding how participants carried out their jobs. Responses were measured according to the following variables: VO = very often; O = often; S = sometimes; N = never; and N/A = not applicable. It also included two open-ended questions that addressed how participants' tasks were conducted and how they used reflection to improve on such tasks. These open-ended questions were also intended to provide further clarification on the quantitative data.

The questionnaire was piloted three times with individuals within the college environment who were not a part of the population surveyed. Those who participated in the pilot were observed and questioned afterwards (Youngman, 1982). A number of changes were made; for example, questions were simplified and some reworded to relate specifically to clerical job functions and to reduce ambiguities.

Follow-up sessions were used to encourage participants to complete the questionnaire and to reflect and expand on answers given to the open-ended questions. The questions are: 'In carrying out the tasks required in your job, what are the steps that you take to ensure that you do your best?, 'List these'; and 'Describe a task that you are required to do on your job. Describe how you are supposed to undertake this task. Have you found a "better" way to do this task? How did you arrive at the "better" way to carry out this task?'

Participants

The participants for the research were in clerical positions in a University College in the Cayman Islands. Thirteen individuals were identified as clerical staff. All but one of the participants were female. Since the focus of this research is about clerical staff, those individuals within the University College who were middle to upper management were excluded.

Data collection methods

Prior to the distribution of the questionnaire, an email was sent to all individuals involved in the research. Since the University College is not very large, 13 questionnaires were hand-delivered to the individuals identified as clerical staff. Individuals were given one week to complete the questionnaire. All questionnaires were collected one week from the date of issuance. Only 10 of the 13 questionnaires were returned, for a completion rate of 77%.

Follow-up sessions were conducted after working hours to establish validity and to reduce and neutralize bias in the data responses given on the survey. The sessions were also used for triangulation (Cresswell, 1994). Triangulation is best done in a quantitative–qualitative study when more than one approach is used to cross-check information; hence, in this case, the open-ended questions and follow-up sessions were used to provide a more complete picture of the responses given by the participants (Gay, Mills, & Airasian, 2009).

Data analysis process

The data were analysed using both quantitative and qualitative procedures. The means and standard deviations were tabulated for each question and responses in the Likert-type scale (Youngman, 1982). The responses to the open-ended questions were analysed for themes or categories (Powell & Renner, 2003), without reference to the results of the quantitative questions results. The categories or themes identified provided a basis for analysis to aid in answering the research question (Gay, Mills & Airasian, 2009).

From this mixed analysis process we constructed an understanding of the clerical staff's use of reflective learning. The results of the analysis are presented in the next section of this paper which summarizes the findings.

Summary of findings

Outcome of Likert-type questions

The study utilized all employees in clerical positions at the University College. Since this is a small college there were 13 individuals who were not classified as management that received the questionnaires. Of the 13 individuals, (12 female and one male), 10 individuals returned the survey, which accounted for a 77% return rate.

The educational level of the participants ranged from some college education to two individuals with master's degrees. A variety of tasks were performed by all the participants, indicative of clerical tasks that would be found in an educational environment. The results of the 10 clerical personnel responses as summarized are shown in Table 1.

Clerical staff use of technical reflective learning

Five questions measured participants' ability to be engaged in technical reflective learning. The overall results indicate that clerical staff in the sample were engaged

Table 1. Reflective learning cluster means and standard deviation (Valli's Typology).

Clusters	N	Minimum	Maximum	Mean	Std deviation
Deliberative reflective learning (DFL)	8	2.50	4.90	3.7858	0.85637
Reflection-on-action (RON)	3	3.70	4.20	4.0000	0.26458
Reflection-in-action (RIN)	4	3.60	4.40	4.0750	0.34034
Personalistic reflection learn (PRF)	4	3.71	4.30	3.9258	0.25945
Critical reflective learning (CFL)	6	3.33	4.20	3.8556	0.38452
Technical reflective learning (TFL)	5	2.89	4.40	3.6514	0.65231

in technical reflective learning when performing routine tasks. The statement 'I think about how well I do my job' was rated the highest in this cluster (mean = 4.4; STD = 0.699). The overall mean for this cluster showed a score of 3.65 and standard deviation of 0.65231 (see Table 1). Participants' responses to the question 'I apply personal beliefs to work-related matters' received the lowest mean score (mean = 2.88). Overall, participants were engaged in technical reflective learning while performing their job tasks.

Clerical staff use of reflection-on-action and reflection-in-action

Reflection-on-action had an overall cluster mean of 4.00, which suggested the second-highest score of all clusters (see Table 1). Participants were engaged in reflection-on-action and often use this form of learning on the job. The results also indicated that reflection-in-action had the highest cluster score of all clusters with a mean of 4.075 (see Table 1) and, like reflection-on-action, participants tended to utilize this type of learning often while performing job tasks.

Clerical staff use of personalistic reflective learning

Personalistic reflective learning had as its highest score an overall mean and standard deviation of 3.93 and 0.61; as a cluster, participants though about their jobs a little less often. The motivation for this reflective stance hinged on their personal growth and was reflected in their response to the statement 'When doing my job, I think about my personal growth'.

Clerical staff use of deliberative reflective learning

Deliberative reflective learning had an overall mean of 3.79 and standard deviation of 0.856. The statement 'When I make decisions, I look for all sides of the situation' received the highest score of all questions (mean = 4.9; STD = 0.316). This suggested that participants very often thought about all 'sides of the story'. Although the highest score was found in this cluster, the lowest was also found here. This indicates that participants made decisions – when it comes to job tasks – that were not based on personal beliefs.

Clerical staff use of critical reflective learning

The questions that fell under this cluster covered how participants thought about the social, moral, political dimensions of their work. Focus was also placed on improving their workplace. There were six questions in this section and the results indicated that clerical staff were more or less concerned with how people were treated in the work environment (mean = 4.2; STD = 1.03).

They were just as concerned about the social and moral dimensions in the workplace (mean = 4.1, 4.1; and STD = 0.876 and 0.876). Thinking about the political dimensions and equal opportunity received the lowest scores in this cluster and variability among responses indicated that they did not quite consider these two issues as often as the other elements. Overall cluster means and standard deviation were, 3.86 and 0.384 respectively, suggesting that while critical reflective learning was important, they thought about their immediate job task most often.

Outcomes for open-ended questions

There were nine responses received for both open-ended questions. These responses were analysed for emerging themes or categories (Powell & Renner, 2003). As a result of analysing the responses, participants were placed in two groups based on themes, phrases or words that emerged from their written responses. Group 1 contained six participants and Group 2 contained three participants.

Analysis indicated that there were clear differentiations in the responses of Group 1 and 2 relating to the first open-ended question about the steps they employed in ensuring that they do their best in carrying out their job tasks. From the analysis of this question, the following themes emerged: check; prioritize; set time frame; review; investigate; implement; translate; create lists; consult; monitor; and ask for feedback. In contrast, participants in Group 2 did not outline steps they took to ensure they did their best in carrying out their job task. Rather, they listed their work-related tasks or gave general comments; for example: '[I] give accurate information to the public'; '[I] always do my job to the best of my ability'; '[I] think about my integrity'.

The differentiation in responses between Groups 1 and 2 blurred when they were asked, in open-ended Question 2, to outline how they could come up with a better way to do their tasks.

Some in Group 1 gave clear examples of reflection upon their work and taking action as a result of such reflection. For example: 'I have decided to use a scanner instead of doing it manually because it is easier and more accurate'; and 'A recent policy that I have written allow(s) me to process refunds more efficiently'. Whilst others were not able to indicate changes that they had made, they reiterated the processes that they use. Group 2 continued their focus on tasks with no indication of reflection and general responses about their work. For example, 'I do my best'; 'I love my work'; 'My job is important to me'.

Having summarized the findings of this study, we now turn our attention to discussing them, thus answering the broad research question 'To what extent do clerical staff at a local university college engage with RL while on the job?'

Discussion

As indicated above, the main aim of the study was to determine the extent to which clerical staff engaged with reflective learning while carrying out their daily job tasks. The study revealed that participants engaged in all types of reflective learning on the job at least at some level and some did this more than others. This finding is not surprising, for Posner (1989) made the point that while reflection is a human attribute, some people engaged in the process more than others. As a result, he coined the phrases 'more-reflective-person' and 'less-reflective-person'.

While this is the case, the study also revealed that, overall, participants tended to engage more often in reflection-on-action (mean = 4.00; STD = 0.264) and reflection-in-action (mean = 4.075; STD = 0.340). This is indicated by the high scores these types of reflection received. This means that participants critically thought about job-related events or situations either before or after they had occurred and, on the spot, in 'the thick of things', as discussed by (Schon, 1983; Adler, 1994). This conclusion is supported by responses to open-ended Question 1, responses such as 'checking', 'reviewing' and 'investigating'. These words are synonymous with actions indicating reflection and specifically reflection-on-action and reflection-in-action. This is so because carrying out these types of reflection requires investigating, checking and reviewing in order to 'frame' problematic issues on the job (Schon, 1983). Responses to open-ended Question 2 also support this conclusion, for to make changes to work-related tasks, as a result of critically thinking about these tasks, involves reflection-in-action and reflection-on-action. For example, participants reported, after reflecting: 'I have decided to use a scanner instead of doing it manually because it is easier and more accurate'; and 'A recent policy that I have written allows me to process refunds more efficiently'.

The next type of reflective learning in which participants most frequently engage is personalistic reflection which had an overall mean = 3.92 and STD = 0.259. However, they did this less than reflection in and on action. This type of reflective learning involves thinking critically about their own personal growth and relationships with colleagues.

Spaulding and Wilson (2002), speaking specifically of teachers, made the point that participants in their study seem to engage more readily and easily with personalistic reflection and continue to do so, even when the researchers tried to get them out of that mode of thinking. Additionally, this occurrence could also indicate a caring disposition among the clerical staff at the University College which is possibly associated with the fact that the majority of participants were females.

Critical reflective learning was engaged in by participants, but with less frequency, as indicated by the following overall scores (mean = 3.85; STD = 0.384). However, some individual aspects of this type of reflection did receive high scores. For example, the fact that participants were extremely concerned about the social and moral dimensions of the workplace (mean = 4.1, 4.1; and STD = 0.876 and 0.876) and about the ways in which people were treated in the workplace (mean = 4.2; STD = 1.03). Overall, the results showed that while this type of learning was important, participants thought more about their immediate job tasks and less about the mission of the organization, planning strategies being employed and the rules of the organization or the political dimensions and issues of equal opportunities on the job.

Deliberative reflective learning which involves thinking about a whole range of on the job concerns did not score high overall, and was also less frequently engaged in (mean = 3.78; STD = 0.856). The lowest scoring reflective learning overall was technical reflection (mean = 3.651; STD = 0.652). This indicates that participants thought less about techniques and skills utilized in carrying out their job tasks or about their own performance or unique work situations and did not apply personal theories to work-related matters.

In conclusion, the extent to which clerical staff engage with reflective learning can be seen in the fact that overall they tended to engage more often in reflection-on-action and reflection-in-action and personalistic reflection. While they did engage in critical and deliberative reflective learning, they did so far less. Technical reflection was the reflective learning type engaged in least by participants. The ability to incorporate best practices in the area of reflection, i.e. reflection-on-action, reflection-in-action, personalistic reflection, critical and deliberative reflective learning and technical reflective learning, is of paramount importance when considering the professional development of both employees and managers. This thought hints at the fact that the results of this study have implications for managers and management. It is to this that we now turn our attention.

Implications for managers and management

The study is very important for several reasons. For, as indicated above, it has implications for professional development of managers and the management process in general and, by extension, for those who work in clerical positions.

Firstly, we suggest that managers need to engage in and encourage their staff's use of reflective learning as a 'cognitive process', for this will benefit both the organization and the individuals in the organization (Hutzschenreuter & Kleindienst, 2006). This is so because RL, when fully understood and applied, leads to greater efficiencies in the workplace. Given employees' adoption of RL as a normal part of their jobs, they can make a valuable contribution to the organization and their contribution, when recognized, can potentially lead to job engagement which ultimately leads to increased satisfaction on the part of the employees.

However, for managers to whole-heartedly encourage the use of RL in the organization and among individual members, they too will need to understand and appreciate the RL process. In other words, they will need to personally experiment with the RL process and apply it to their daily tasks. Our study provides a useful starting point for developing this understanding and appreciation for RL.

Secondly, while this, to some extent, depends on the individual worker's willingness, we see the manager's role as helping to facilitate or move the staff towards becoming reflective practitioners (Schön, 1983). The benefit of this process includes staff adopting a self-directed professional development stance (Minott, 2010b) and members of staff who are reflective practitioners could also engage in critical thinking about workplace issues, thus leading to greater understanding of the intricacies of their work tasks and the continuous improvement of their work.

Thirdly, managers' personal engagement with, and whole-hearted encouragement of, RL could enable them to become conversant with two types of knowledge in use in the organization, i.e. tacit knowledge (the belief that knowledge is essentially personal in nature and is therefore difficult to extract from the heads of individuals) and explicit knowledge (the understanding that knowledge can be explained by individuals – even though some effort and assistance may be required to help individuals articulate what they know) (Sanchez, 2000). Tapping into tacit knowledge could help managers fill in any gaps between what employees are expected to do and what they actually do. This could also lead to organizational learning which, in essence, leads to better ways of doing job tasks (Clegg, Kornberger, & Pitsis, 2008).

Fourthly, managers who are cognizant of the process of RL would also be aware of its potential to aid in accomplishing strategic goals in the organization and this awareness may even have implications for staff performance review processes.

Further research

The findings of our study in no way exhaust the findings on reflective learning and small organizations. Since the literature review indicated sparse information about the use of reflective learning in the business context, our study can be considered exploratory in nature. There are a number of studies in the academic or educational environment (Minott 2009, 2010a; Zeichner & Liston, 1996). These studies embrace reflective learning as a tool to aid continuous improvement in an educational context.

Given the restrictive nature of our research, the following recommendations are made: (1) Research could be done on a much larger sample that include both male and female clerical workers and a comparison made on how both carry out job tasks in a reflective manner; and (2) Another questionnaire – based on Valli's typology of reflection – could be developed to measure how managers of clerical workers aid them in carrying out their daily job tasks.

Limitations of the study

The aims of the investigation were achieved. This study also provides readers with a quick view into the functioning of a small organization. This is important because it seems the area of reflective learning in small firms, businesses or organizations is under-studied internationally and certainly in the context of the Cayman Islands, where there is no known research addressing this area.

Having said this, we will state that, by pointing out the degree to which participants engaged with reflective learning on the job, we were able to make relatively general statements in this regard. However, given the nature of the research in which we engaged, large-scale generalization was neither appropriate nor was it the outcome we sought. However, while this study provided findings that might be similarly obtained from like groups and situations elsewhere, and sufficient details of the research context, data collection and analysis provided, we leave our readers to make their own judgments about transferability to other settings.

Readers should also consider that the study covered a number of areas that could easily form the core concerns for separate case studies. In this study, these complex areas have been examined from a narrow empirical perspective – that is, 13 respondents – and from our own organization. However, given the short time frame and our limited financial resources, this narrow focus made the study both manageable and achievable.

Since the study relied on self-reports and descriptive information, respondents had to rely on memory recollections of past events or situations. This provided room for important details to be left out, withheld and subjected to the problems inherent to memory such as memory loss and distortion. Because of these factors, the data presented were a reflection of what the respondents remembered and chose to disclose. The results, therefore, were also not necessarily full and complete accounts of events or situations the respondents recounted. In addition, it was not within the scope of the study to corroborate accounts of events or situations described by the respondents.

References

Adler, S. (1994). Reflective practice and teacher education. In Ross E. Wayne (Ed.), *Reflective practice in social studies* (pp. 49–56). Washington, DC: National Council for the Social Studies.

Boyd, E.M., & Fales, A.W. (1983). Reflective learning: Key to learning from experience. *Journal of Humanistic Psychology, 23*(2), 99–117.

Brockbank, A., & McGill, I. (2007). *Facilitating reflective learning in higher education* (2nd Ed.). Maidenhead: Open University Press.

Clegg, S., Kornberger, M., & Pitsis, T. (2008). *Managing & organizations: An introduction to theory and practice*. Los Angeles, CA: Sage.

Cresswell, J.W. (1994). *Research design: Qualitative and quantitative approaches*. Thousand Oaks, CA: Sage.

Cummings, O.W. (2009). Admins, then and now. *OfficePRO, 69*(8), 12–15.

De Dea Roglio, K., & Light, G. (2009). Executive MBA programs: The development of the reflective executive. *Academy of Management Learning & Education, 8*(2), 156–173.

Degree Directory. (2010). *What is clerical work?* Retrieved from http://degreedirectory.org/articles/What_is_Clerical_Work.html.

Farrell, T.S.C. (2001). Tailoring reflection to individual needs: A TESOL case study. *Journal of Education for Teaching, 27*(1), 23–38.

Fowler, B. (1996). *Critical thinking across the curriculum project 'definitions of critical thinking'.* Lee's Summit, MO: Longview Community College. Retrieved from http://www.kcmetro.cc.mo.us/longview/ctac/definitions.htm.

Gay, L.R., Mills, G.E., & Airasian, P. (2009). *Educational research: Competencies for analysis and applications* (9th ed.). Upper Saddle River, NJ: Pearson.

Ghaye, T., & Ghaye, K. (1999). *Teaching and learning through critical reflective practice.* London: David Fulton.

Hatton, N., & Smith, D. (1995). Facilitating reflection; Issues and research. *Forum of Education, 50*(1), 49–65.

Hutzschenreuter, T., & Kleindienst, I. (2006). Strategy-process research: What have we learned and what is still to be explored. *Journal of Management, 32*(5), 673–720.

Minott, M.A. (2009). *Reflection and reflective teaching, a case study of four seasoned teachers in the Cayman Islands.* Saarbrücken, Germany: VDM Verlag Dr. Müller.

Minott, M.A. (2010a). *Reflective teaching: Properties, tool, benefits and support.* Saarbrücken, Germany: VDM Verlag Dr. Müller.

Minott, M.A. (2010b). Reflective teaching as self-directed professional development: Building practical or work-related knowledge. *Professional Development in Education, 36*(1), 325–338.

Munro, J., & Cook, R. (2008). The small enterprise as the authentic learning environment opportunity (SEALEO). *Aslib Proceedings, 60*(6), 686–700.

Oliver, J. (2006). Developing a service management strategy facilitated by action learning: An empirical study from the UK health & fitness industry. *Action Learning: Research and Practice, 3*(2), 213–220.

Pennypacker, J. (2009). *Clerical duties.* Retrieved from http://www.ehow.com/facts_5217815_clerical-duties.html.

Posner, G.J. (1989). *Field experience methods of reflective teaching.* New York: Longman.

Powell, E.T., & Renner, M. (2003). *Analyzing qualitative data.* Retrieved from http://cecommerce.uwex.edu/pdfs/G3658_12.PDF.

Sanchez, R. (2000). *'Tacit knowledge' versus 'explicit knowledge' approaches to knowledge management practice.* Retrieved from http://www.knowledgeboard.com/download/3512/Tacit-vs-Explicit.pdf.

Schon, D.A. (1983). *Reflective practitioner.* New York: Basic Books.

Schon, D.A. (1987). *Educating the reflective practitioner.* San Francisco, USA: Jossey-Bass.

Smith, J. (2010). *Clerical support functions.* Retrieved from http://www.ehow.com/list_6695066_clerical-support-functions.html.

Smith, M.K. (2001). Donald Schön: learning, reflection and change, *The encyclopedia of informal education.* Retrieved from http://www.infed.org/thinkers/et-schon.htm.

Spaulding, E., & Wilson, A. (2002). Demystifying reflection: A study of pedagogical strategies that encourage reflective journal writing. *Teachers College Record, 104*(7), 1393–1421.

Valli, L. (1997). Listening to other voices: A description of teacher reflection in the United States. *Peabody journal of Education, 72*(1), 67–88.

Van Manen, M. (1995). On the epistemology of reflective practice. *Teachers and Teaching; Theory and Practice, 1*, 33–50.

Youngman, M.B. (1982). Rediguide 12 Designing and Analysing Questionnaires. Oxford: University of Nottingham.

Zeichner, K.M., & Liston, D.P. (Eds.). (1996). *Reflective teaching – an introduction.* Mahwah, New Jersey, USA: Lawrence Erlbaun.

Wikis: building a learning experience between academe and businesses

Keith Halcro and Anne M.J. Smith

Caledonian Business School, Glasgow Caledonian University, Glasgow, UK

This article represents the second article in a series evaluating wikis as an educational tool, having previously researched students' perspectives of wikis as a learning tool. The aim of this second instalment was to evaluate the experience of not only MBA students but also entrepreneurs and academics of wikis as a learning tool. Throughout the research the participants were encouraged to reflect and discuss their learning experience with one another in order to assess the strengths and weaknesses of wikis as an educational tool. Qualitative oral and written data gained during and after the teaching reflected this experience has been a positive one for students, staff and entrepreneurs. The entrepreneurs have been particularly enthusiastic about the results, citing the educational and managerial benefits to their businesses. Evidence, however, also reveals that on reflection some of the processes and procedures need to be adapted and amended to gain greater initial student buy-in. The recurring criticism that academe and business too often fail to translate their relationships into practical outcomes can be rebutted through the development and application of wikis. Wikis offer different, but complimentary results for the various stakeholders. It is an innovative, low-cost technological tool that integrates entrepreneurial and experiential learning. It allows students and staff to understand and explore in real time issue(s) confronting small and medium enterprises, whilst business can access contemporary knowledge and practice at minimal cost.

Introduction

This article is the second in a series examining the use and application of wikis as a learning tool to enhance entrepreneurial knowledge, develop technical skills and increase employability skills amongst honours year and MBA students. The first article evaluated three different honours and MBA student cohorts' experiences in relation to these themes. This article seeks to develop this thinking and understanding by examining these themes from the perspectives of entrepreneurs, academic staff and MBA students, through the development of three wikis for three micro-businesses. The decision to use wikis reflected a number of philosophical and pedagogical issues. Philosophically, the teaching team was keen to strengthen its ties with local entrepreneurs, a desire shared by the university and one arguably pursued by many universities. This desire aligns with pedagogical arguments about the need to more closely integrate business and academe, and finds recurrent expression in higher education literature and policy (Cambridge Report, 2007), but also employers' criticisms that students need greater exposure to the thinking and practices of organisational life (Financial Services Skills Council, 2010). These criticisms argue students need to develop academically and socially, using a variety of pedagogical mechanisms, including collaborative projects. The conundrum facing universities is the drive to deliver this experience efficiently and effectively. It is these demands that encouraged the teaching team to look beyond traditional lectures and consider wikis as a tool for entrepreneurship teaching, learning and assessment; a tool viewed as benefitting students and staff alike in creating a better pedagogical experience (Cronin, 2009; McCarthy, Smith, &DeLuca, 2010; Wheeler, Yeomans, & Wheeler, 2008).

Initially, the literature discusses ideas emerging amongst entrepreneurial education to contextualise current pedagogical practice and thinking, especially the thinking surrounding a constructivist teaching and learning approach. This approach encourages students to reflect critically on processes and industry applicability, and is a key tenet of the university's MBA programme. Discussion subsequently reviews the roles Web 2.0 and, in particular, wikis are playing in teaching, learning and assessment. The 'newness' of this medium coupled with a constructivist teaching approach encouraged the researchers to adopt action research as a methodology. The results of the data collected from this approach are coded thematically to explain the findings in relation to extant literature and to advocate the value of Wikis in meeting the demands of pedagogical and financial efficiency and effectiveness.

Literature review

It is argued that entrepreneurship education is dynamic and complex (Smith, Halcro, & Chalmers, 2009); an issue Pittaway and Cope (2007a) sought to clarify through a systematic literature review, by theming ideas and identifying research gaps. Citing National Council for Graduate Entrepreneurship research, Pittaway and Cope (2007a) repeated the claim that entrepreneurship education has impacted significantly on British universities, but they believed that there still existed room for improvement in developing a better understanding and ordering of entrepreneurship education. This belief centred on the evidence that entrepreneurship education varies in style and content; features Mwasalwiba (2010) states characterise global entrepreneurship education. Nonetheless, Huebscher and Lendner (2010) posit entrepreneurship education requires dynamic interaction in which the focus should be opportunity recognition and decision-making, ideally within a framework that involves students and entrepreneurs in a mutual exchange of knowledge. These observations support Bumpus and Burton's (2008) comment that it is ultimately incumbent on educators to create effective learning opportunities for entrepreneur students. The concern, though, is that in order to involve entrepreneurs in the learning experience, academics need to better understand the under-researched topic of how entrepreneurs learn (Xiao, Marino, & Zhuang, 2010); an issue Collins, Smith, and Hannon (2006) lament is poorly understood. It is acknowledged, however, that entrepreneurs value knowledge and actively scan the environment seeking tools to lever out this resource, often using tools that are noted for their practicality (Taylor,

Jones, & Boles, 2004). This use of practical, often informal, mechanisms such as networks (Foss 2010) exemplifies the action learning favoured by entrepreneurs (Rae, 2000; Rae & Carswell, 2000).

Numerous writers believe this view of entrepreneurial learning reflects the reality that entrepreneurial learning is a mixture of experiential learning, reflective practice and social interaction (Rae, 2000; Cope & Watts, 2000; Pittaway & Cope, 2007a, 2007b; Smith & Paton, 2011). Smith and Paton (2011), in an international study of nascent entrepreneurs, highlighted reflective practice as a building block in developing self efficacy and improving general self-confidence in students' learning process. Fusing these two themes of entrepreneurship education and entrepreneurial learning offers scope for further study, particularly as Gibb's (cited in Collins, Smith, & Hannon, 2006) contention of a generation ago still holds true that business students are taught in an overly academic manner that emphasises analysis, rather than an action approach experienced and favoured by many entrepreneurs; an approach students similarly favour (Huebscher & Lendner, 2010). Mwasalwiba (2010) saw these ideas coalescing in a number of questions on the methods and experiences students and entrepreneurs encountered. His critique queried ideas about the applied teaching methods used and the relevance entrepreneurship education offers to local entrepreneurs. Answers to these questions have suggested technology can play a critical role in enhancing the educational experience, claiming that technology allows greater connectivity, flexibility and engagement (McCarthy, Smith, & DeLuca, 2010; Wood, 2010). The promises offered by technology have led academics to view Web 2.0 as an educational solution, particularly as Minocha (2009) wryly states many students are conversant with the technology. She argues that since students produce content willingly for social interaction, it can by extension be used to develop a more student-centred approach.

This thinking emphasises that the students' experiences stimulate learning through shared activities in action-led environments and this process helps to build new knowledge through successive refinement (Levy & Hadar, 2010). Arguably, this approach corresponds to constructivist teaching and learning theory (Hearn, Foth, & Gray, 2008), which suggests communicating and collaborating within a network develops individual and collective knowledge and skills; thus, the focus of the learning process becomes one of student enquiry, rather than lecturer-centred. Central to this learning process was the realisation that students and the entrepreneurs needed to reflect periodically on their learning experiences (Pittaway & Cope, 2007b). Hatton and Smith (1995) viewed reflection as operating over four stages: technical; descriptive; dialogic; and critical. Crucially, these stages represent a progressively more demanding, sophisticated analysis of the experience. Klenowski and Lunt (2007) contend this deepening process helps to move reflective learning beyond the criticism that reflective learning is simply a mechanism that scrutinises and seeks to enhance personal and organisational development. Taylor, Jones and Boles (2004) maintain networks can further deepen the reflective process through players collectively monitoring, stimulating and supporting each other, to create a community of practice. This emphasis on interactive collaboration correlates ideally to the principles and practices found with Web 2.0 (Cronin, 2009; Levy & Hadar, 2010).

Cronin (2009) acknowledges an agreed definition of Web 2.0 is missing, but he believes that many people understand the term and realise Web 2.0 encompasses technologies such as social networking sites, blogs, mashups, RSS, folksonomies and wikis. He claims Web 2.0 has fundamentally changed the way the Web is used, a belief Hartshorne and Ajjan (2009) suggest lies in the user's ability to produce and control his/her own data and information. This is too simple an explanation. It is as Ma and Yuen (2008) emphasise the collaborative, social interaction that has helped to popularise Web 2.0, a characteristic they suggest endears itself as a learning tool. The interactive nature of these technologies encourages the user to draw on knowledge accessible via the World Wide Web and engage in knowledge exchange with invited users or publically accessible sources such as Wikipedia (Wheeler, Yeomans, & Wheeler, 2008). Educationalists believe this strength provides a platform for students' work (Levy & Hadar, 2010) and therefore enables material to be effectively and efficiently critiqued and improved by colleagues or potentially the wider networked community. The students' awareness of 'self' and their 'public' contribution means that reflective thinking is deepened, because other users scrutinise the material. It is also evident that allowing students to observe and reflect on 'others' contributions enables students to evaluate the strengths and weaknesses of others relative to themselves, thereby creating a strong learning dynamic within a community of practitioners. This dynamic encourages a more reflective learning approach, for it allows the learners to visualise and examine other users' content and helps to move the learner towards a more critical understanding of themselves, their environment and their relationships (Klenowski & Lunt, 2007). It can also be suggested that this approach fosters social connectivity and a collaborative environment, each considered important by constructivist theorists in establishing effective teaching and learning environments (Hartshorne & Ajjan, 2009; Smith & Paton, 2011).

The success of Web 2.0 relies on understanding and creating a shared philosophy based on openness, trust and communication; in effect, the attributes of any successful network. The role networks play in learning has been discussed at considerable length (Cheng, 2005; Borzsony & Hunter,1996), and it is claimed that technology can play an invaluable role in stimulating and sustaining these networks (Mlitwa, 2007); however, central to this success is the need to build trust, a feature that literature repeatedly argues is necessary if players are to access rare and valuable knowledge and thereby gain competitive advantage (Bergh, Thorgren, & Wincent, 2011).

Wikis are a collaborative project which draw on a number of relevant Web hyperlinks to help illustrate an idea or story. Wood (2010) stated the purpose of a wiki is to build a shared repository of information on a common topic, a view that finds expression amongst other writers (Cronin, 2009; Levy & Hadar, 2010). The subtext to this process is collaboration, one that contrasts the individualism of a blog. This collaborative process has led some (Cole, 2008, p. 142) to claim that it can be viewed as 'a tool for building communities of practice', a potential benefit recognised by many firms (Hendrix, 2007). This potential benefit may explain Cerny's observation (cited in Cronin, 2009) that half of all companies in the United States would be using wikis by the end of 2009, although both writers state the reality is that many firms have only limited understanding of the technology, its application and development. The organisational benefits, though, have started to emerge in terms of learning (Hendrix, 2007; McKelvie, Dotska, & Patrick, 2007) and marketing (Hearn et al., 2008).

The lure of wikis' affordability harnessed to the power of the World Wide Web offers commercial and academic promise, particularly as it allows users access to what is essentially an infinite knowledge source. Wikis are probably best known through the Wikipedia website (http://www.wikipedia.org), which allows users to create, share and edit information remotely about topics of mutual interest at minimal cost. Some critics, however, have expressed concerns relating to monitoring and validity of some content (McKiernan, 2005), but it is evident wikis can quickly build on existing knowledge to disseminate expanded knowledge. Empirical studies of wikis in teaching and learning are revealing similar patterns. Chu (2008) investigated and developed wiki software for journalist students and concluded that students enjoyed the experience, citing particularly the collaborative benefits to be gained from working on projects online.

The evidence indicates that there is a growing body of literature highlighting wiki creation as a positive learning experience (Cronin, 2009; Laff, 2007; Wood, 2010). In terms of entrepreneurship education, the focus should now consider the combination and interplay of wiki literature with the arguably more developed understanding of creating entrepreneurial learning environments (Anderson & Jack, 2008; Mwasalwiba, 2010). The question has to be asked: can wikis provide entrepreneurship education with a pedagogical and financial tool that can effectively and efficiently deliver and enhance teaching, learning and assessment? The following methodological section will describe how wikis were implemented.

Methodology

This study drew on qualitative data (Silverman, 2006) to explore the participants' opinions and experiences in developing three business wikis. The nature and problem of the research favoured an action research approach, since firstly the teaching and learning strategy was a constructivist approach rooted in the idea that learning would occur through participation and experience. Secondly the 'newness' of the technology (Cronin, 2009) involved the stakeholders, students, entrepreneurs and staff continually diagnosing, planning, acting on and evaluating their experiences and decisions through a spiralling, reflective approach. This processional language aligns strongly to the precepts of action research, particularly when it involves teams researching and progressively solving problems (Dickens & Watkins, 1999; Kemmis & McTaggart, 2000; Raelin, 1999). Comparable studies (Desmarais et al., 2008; Jackson, 2010) have adopted a similar stance grounded in the argument that action research is suitable when examining problem-solving issues. In fact, Hearn, Foth and Gray's (2008) research demonstrated the symmetry between action research and its emphasis on problem-solving, whilst using a constantly evolving technology, Web 2.0, which requires ongoing solutions.

Data were collected from the participants (11 students, three entrepreneurs and two academics) in the form of written reports (self-reflective reports and emails), interviews and informal oral feedback and then analysed to identify and categorise themes (Silverman, 2006). A comparative analysis of the academics, entrepreneurs and MBA students' comments enabled the researchers to view and examine collectively, then separately, the three stakeholders' perspectives. This procedure allowed a two-layered analysis, by revealing both overall themes, but also themes relevant to each stakeholder, as clearly each stakeholder has different requirements.

Implementing the research

The researchers selected the three entrepreneurs based on a matrix of attributes: the participants' attitude towards openness to new ideas; a willingness to collaborate with a university, particularly in sharing potentially sensitive company information; and finally the validity of the 'problem'. Entrepreneur A was contacted through a third party, a consultancy company that deals widely with innovation ready companies in Scotland. The company referred Entrepreneur A, stating the entrepreneur possessed an interest in lifelong learning. By contrast, Entrepreneurs B and C were known previously to the researchers, since they had been variously involved in the university's activities, including guest lectures to students on various aspects of entrepreneurship. The three entrepreneurs were contacted and asked to participate in setting a problem for MBA students that could be addressed through the creation of a wiki page. The research would run from January through to May. Following their agreement, the entrepreneurs provided a proforma brief describing the organisation, the nature of the problem and the outcome the entrepreneur sought. The briefs were then edited and agreed by the academics and entrepreneurs. This process of reflection and discussion helped to strengthen the degree of trust between the two stakeholders, which was critical because the briefs discussed sensitive organisational information. Brunetto and Farr-Wharton (2007) comment that revealing such information makes participants vulnerable and therefore the players need to be assured by the other players' motives and conduct. Part of this surety involved the academics and subsequently the students signing non-disclosure forms, but it was clear that the briefs were critical to the research's success. Following Cole's (2008) strictures, the briefs sought to establish an understandable but short set of achievable aims and objectives. Once all parties had agreed the final briefs, they were posted on their own project page in wikispaces. The collaborative nature of the project meant that the entrepreneurs and academics could see and comment on the solutions.

The research drew on Smith, Halcro and Chalmers's (2009) experience to inform the participants' actions and reinforces the notion that this research reflects part of a continuum. Problems encountered by Smith, Halcro and Chalmers (2009) led the team to create a workbook containing a number of problem-solving exercises. This process encouraged the student to reflect on the transferability of the skills and knowledge in developing wiki pages. In a three-hour session students were organised into groups of three to four, with the academic playing a facilitating role, as recommended in constructivist theory (Hearn et al., 2008). The introduction of the workbook aligned to Hatton and Smith's (1995) tactic which had focused on developing students' technical skills and confidence, before subsequently describing and critically evaluating their own and others' skills. This process allowed the students to deepen their understanding of their own strengths and weaknesses. Following completion of these activities, the students focused on identifying and defining the problem. At this point several issues arose. It was clear that the brevity of the briefs had resulted in the students struggling to empathise with the companies, the nature of their activities and the landscape in which they operated. This weakness, a lack of context, haunted the opening weeks as students grappled to understand the companies' requirements, in particular Company E (Entrepreneur C). This software company's brief had identified the need for market research on potential customers for one of their products, an online focus group capability. Paradoxically, this concept of an online focus group did not resonate with the students, yet the students had industry experience and in some cases direct experience of focus groups. This inability to relate to the issue was not isolated to Company E (Entrepreneur C), since lack of context similarly slowed development of Companies D and F's wiki pages. Company D, a tourism business, had outlined the problem that the company wished to offer cycling holidays, but needed to identify agents in Europe to sell these holidays. Students thought the brief was asking for agents to supply holidays. The third company, owned by Entrepreneur B, offered a highly innovative safety product for extreme sports events, but again students struggled with the concept of the product and the objective, which was to identify sponsorship opportunities. These issues required clarification. The academics' belief that focusing on brevity would make the projects clearer and more manageable had resulted in difficulties of contextualisation.

The result was the students' enthusiasm waned, the entrepreneurs appeared bemused and the academics became frustrated. These difficulties subsided as the three stakeholders began to more enthusiastically communicate with one another. The result was that the participants reflected on how to understand and solve the problems. This experience supported the validity of adopting an action research approach, since the iterative learning process and experimental nature of the technology meant it was an evolving, problem-solving exercise (Chen et al., 2005). Solution one was to encourage the students and entrepreneurs to use the technology to communicate, by querying and questioning each other regarding issues and processes. The resulting email traffic clarified the context and problem, but importantly helped to build trust and establish the understanding that there were reciprocal benefits (Bergh et al., 2011). Klenowski and Lunt (2007) argue that reflecting on this outcome enables participants to appreciate the consequences of their actions on self and the wider group. The entrepreneurs realised that specialist knowledge existed amongst the students which could improve organisational performance, while the students came to appreciate the complexities and challenges faced by entrepreneurs. This better understanding resulted in improved wiki development. The second solution involved more direct academic intervention, by creating and posing a set of related tasks for each project; for example, Company E's page was improved by introducing questions that required the students to research linkages and practices between comparable companies' websites and social network sites. This helped to clarify the problem, but the closed, directional nature of the questions changed the process, making it less collaborative and more task-driven. A further solution lay in examining and discussing the wikis produced by previous cohorts to assess their relative strengths and weaknesses and adopt elements of good practice, a feature Hartshorne and Ajjan (2009) identify as part of the constructivist dialogue and which returns to a theme identified by Klenowski and Lunt (2007) that reflective learning has to involve critical evaluation of what has occurred and what needs to be remedied. These examples increased the students' confidence in their own ability and resulted in a number of adaptations and refinements to the wikis. This more activist intervention by the academics and increased communication between students and entrepreneurs saw the development of more robust, better quality work, but written and oral feedback from the three stakeholders revealed generic, as well as specific, issues, which in part mirrored Smith, Halcro and Chalmers's (2009) study, but also threw up issues previously unknown.

Discussion

Data analysis revealed generic and specific issues. Collectively, all stakeholders positively reiterated the previous literature's comments highlighting the two themes:

ease of use and pedagogical value as a learning tool. However, all participants identified the problem of communication at the outset of the project. Specific stakeholder problems included instrumental thinking (students) and technical skills (entrepreneurs), both of which could be ascribed to the pressure of other commitments. The problems encountered ultimately, though, required the academics to re-evaluate their role if a constructivist approach was to succeed.

The previously circulated, positive messages about wWikis' role as a knowledge resource (Hartshorne & Ajjan, 2009) again found expression amongst the stakeholders. It was noticeable also that many of the MBA students recognised from the outset the benefits a wiki offered in terms of knowledge sharing and accessibility, whether on or off campus. These benefits stretched to the product's transferability from academe to the workplace:

> The use of the wiki for collaborative working and knowledge sharing for the module was a great idea. I am familiar with a number of tools used for this purpose and had introduced them to the organisation where I was working. (Student 1)

This reflective process highlighting the applicability of classroom knowledge and practice to the workplace undoubtedly spurred a more critical appreciation of the wikis' value, and echoed an enthusiasm amongst the 2009 part-time MBA cohort, who had similarly recognised the potential workplace benefits (Smith et al., 2009). This positive theme existed amongst some of the 2010 cohort (Students 4 and 9) from the beginning; for example, Student 4 identified the wiki's use in capturing his organisation's tacit knowledge amongst retiring engineers. He argued this knowledge would be invaluable in succession planning and acting as repository of shared information, ideas that mirror Wood's (2010) definition and Cole's (2008) view that wikis can build communities of practice. A more widespread enthusiasm stemmed from the ease in developing a wiki (Students 4, 6 and 11), a view previously articulated amongst MBA students (Smith et al., 2009) and tallies with other studies such as Chu's (2008) observations of journalism students. This technical ease paralleled another previously identified benefit: the ability to work on the wiki remotely, unconstrained by location or time of day, a benefit Entrepreneur C observed:

> The mobility of today's communications allows for a 'snatched' five minutes here or there, for example on the train and the wiki lends itself totally to this type of working.

Several students (Students 4,10 and 11) expressed similar opinions which again reiterate Smith, Halcro and Chalmers's (2009) earlier findings, as well as other studies (Chu, 2008; Cronin, 2009) that the benefit of using a technology based on the Web gives the user control (Hartshorne & Ajjan 2009) and supports Minocha's (2009) belief that Web 2.0 technology can put the student at the centre of the learning process. This ability to constantly interact with the learning process undoubtedly enables the student to engage in an iterative process of learning that reflects Kolb's Learning Cycle (1984) and enables the learner to review his/her practices, but also to reflect critically of those of his/her colleagues and thus reinforce a sense of a community of practice. These benefits underpin the value of a constructivist approach to teaching and learning, from both students' and entrepreneurs' perspectives, but also the academics in employing an understandable, accessible technology that allows the student to drive the learning process. The value of this technology increased when the students recognised its transferability to another setting; for example, the workplace. Knowles (2005) suggests this connection is particularly forceful when experienced by adult learners. This experience of developing and evaluating ideas and solutions to the issues allowed all the stakeholders to develop as reflective practitioners (Harsthorne & Ajjan, 2009). This was most explicit amongst the students and lecturers, since a cornerstone of the MBA's learning and teaching strategy was the concept of the 'reflective manager' rooted in Argyris and Schön's (1974) ideas of critical reflection. The repeated practice and discussion of reflection throughout the MBA programme helped the students and lecturers to overcome many of the difficulties and evaluate the value of wikis as a learning tool. Student 6 perhaps most succinctly reflected that wikis had been 'hugely' beneficial in creating a better understanding of their (the students') potential and, implicitly, their role in their future learning. This opinion subscribes to the principle that reflection is invaluable in developing the learner's scope for further learning (Rae, 2000; Rae & Carswell, 2000).

The positive observations noted about knowledge-sharing, transferability and ease of use and access contrasted the comments arising from difficulties of poor communication. These problems are often magnified by group work (Tuckman, 1965), particularly ones involving international students (Hyland, Trahar, Anderson, & Dickens, 2008). In hindsight, the academics realise that a weak rapport emerged between the entrepreneurs and the students and consequently promoted Tuckman's (1965) and Hyland et al.'s (2008) observations. This situation arose because, at the outset, there was no physical contact between these two stakeholders. This lack of connectivity was reinforced by the brevity of the brief. Too many of the students had little empathy for the concept, as they could not visualise or understand the entrepreneurs and consequently trust failed to emerge; a key theme in developing a community of practice (Pack, 2011; Taylor et al., 2004). This need to understand context, process and purpose is recognised as important (Cole, 2008; Cronin, 2009; Smith et al., 2009), hence the preparatory three-hour session. This workshop had aimed to create a sense of understanding and familiarisation prior to the students developing the content, but it is acknowledged that the presence of the entrepreneurs at the outset to answer queries would have avoided some of the uncertainty and ignorance that initially bedevilled the wiki projects. The reality is that humans often require stakeholder interaction to resolve organisational problems (Halcro, 2008) and develop trust (Brunetto & Farr-Wharton (2007). These issues cannot always be successfully remedied by technology, since it struggles to capture and convey the nuances and complexities inherent in many problem scenarios. Arguably, the intervention of the lecturers to force the students to more critically review and explain their processes and practices resolved the queries, but this action generated a time lag and resulted in diminished student and entrepreneur interest, particularly against a backdrop of their other demands. This issue manifest itself in two part-time students' comments and behaviour. These students explained that because the wiki was not assessed, they felt little incentive to participate, particularly given the demands of their working lives and the pressures of writing their dissertation. This instrumental approach to learning is frequently noted (Ecclestone, 2007; Karabenick and Knapp, 1991; Ottewill, 2003). Intriguingly, written feedback subsequently disclosed that layered over this attitude was the belief group work requires time and effort, resources the students were not prepared to sacrifice, given the outcome was not assessed:

At this time, due to other pressures in my life I only wanted to focus on what was required to pass the course. (Student 15)

The perceived effort required became inflated in some students' eyes by the fact that the groups involved international students, a group with which literature suggests domestic students often dislike collaborating, because of cultural and language issues (Hyland et al., 2008). Ironically, as time passed a number of the British students expressed their contrition, saying that the international students contributed disproportionately to the wikis and acknowledged the missed opportunities for their own learning from their limited input (Students 2, 6 and 7):

I personally should have taken the opportunity to learn from the international students, rather than wait for it to happen. (Student 7)

This thinking became more apparent following discussions on the role of networks as a source of competitive advantage. The realisation then dawned amongst the British students that the international students offered a source of knowledge for entry and/or development of their home country's markets. This may appear self-evident in hindsight, but the instrumental approach adopted by some part-time British students, especially in their reticence to engage with international students in group working, damaged their own learning and potentially opportunities for their organisations. Ironically, the international students empathised with this behaviour, rationalising that since part-time students were also full-time employees it made sense to manage one's limited resources, particularly since the wiki was formative.

The entrepreneurs observed this lack of motivation may explain the communication problems, but tellingly Entrepreneur A stated 'all parties have an onus to communicate effectively to ensure an accurate result'. This reflection identifies the reality that the learner has to understand how his/her behaviour impacts on the network and remedy any behavioural issues if they are to understand and develop as a reflective learner (Klenowski & Lunt, 2007). This observation also acknowledges the role everyone plays in creating a successful wiki and the elements necessary to underpin constructivist learning; as Janasz and Forret (2007) state, good communication requires openness, trust and honesty. One could further argue the elements that glue together the network need to be evident amongst all actors, as some of the entrepreneurs were similarly guilty of poor communication.

Two of the Entrepreneurs (A and B) admitted only during post-module feedback that their weak technical skills and pressures of business discouraged them from monitoring the wikis more effectively and communicating issues with students and academics. Their possible embarrassment at these technical failings may explain their reticence in providing feedback and suggests that, like many learners, their learning approach is focused on the needs of the moment on which there is a discernible, immediate payback. Their behaviour echoed the earlier comments about the instrumental approach of two of the part-time students (Ecclestone, 2007; Karabenick & Knapp, 1991; Ottewill, 2003). This observation suggests an area worthy of further discussion and aligns to Xiao, Marino and Zhuang's (2010) argument that there is a need to better understand entrepreneurs' learning process, particularly if further wiki development is to involve entrepreneurs.

On reflection, the academics were also guilty of mistakes by focusing overly on the student experience because of their proximity. It is recognised that the academics should have engaged the entrepreneurs more actively, particularly in trying to assess the entrepreneurs' learning style through the guise of learning by doing, experiential formats and activity (Rae, 2000; Rae & Carswell, 2000; Cope & Watts, 2000; Pittaway & Cope, 2007b). The evidence suggests, however, that the entrepreneurs did gain a better understanding of the wikis' potential and the university's willingness to interact and support the business community. The academics acknowledge that while the students had a strong theoretical and applied understanding of self-reflection, this was more weakly rooted amongst the entrepreneurs and only emerged clearly late on in the study, following discussions and suggestions from students and academics when the entrepreneurs' critically acknowledged their technical limitations and laxity in communicating. Their reflective comments acknowledged the success and potential of the wikis, but also a sense that the opportunity had not been fully exploited. This realisation has prompted the teaching team to consider more critically from the outset the various stakeholders' educational and technical knowledge and if necessary consider a more interventionist approach in developing some of the fundamental technical and pedagogical skills. The research has previously cited entrepreneurs' preference for practical, action-orientated methods (Pittaway & Cope 2007b), and therefore solutions need to consider these features; one solution may lie in using a journal. This mechanism has been cited widely in developing reflective practice, for example, amongst university students, health professionals and educationalists (Husu, Toom, & Patrikainen, 2008; Mann, Gordon, & MacLeod, 2009; Morrison, 1996). A journal in the guise of a blog could offer a vehicle for publishing problems and the journey in developing possible solutions to these problems.

The involvement of this third group in this iteration, entrepreneurs, has created a more complex set of relationships, which is inevitable as a network grows (Rowley, 1997). The learning expectation had initially viewed the students and entrepreneurs collaborating in the development of three wikis, facilitated by the actions of the academics. This scenario envisaged a tripartite collaboration, but one arguably student-centred and driven by the practices of Kolb's (1984) Learning Cycle. The emergence of the academics as the nexus of the relationships, in which they directed rather than facilitated the learning process, runs contrary to the constructivist approach (Chen et al., 2005). This outcome arose because of a variety of factors: the academics' knowledge of both stakeholders and their prior technical knowledge, coupled with issues of motivation amongst some participants, required the academics to review and initially adapt a learning and teaching approach, from one of facilitating to one of directing. The academics' view was that this was neither desirable nor sustainable if all stakeholders were to understand the potential benefits of using a wiki. As solutions emerged through collective reflection, the lecturers' role reverted to one of facilitation and encouraging the students to reflect on their experiences to develop collectively solutions, but also, where appropriate, individual solutions to their own unique learning needs. The experience has forced the academics to undoubtedly re-evaluate the approaches and processes required to sustain and develop the idea of using in the future remotely located organisations where face-to-face relationships with students is simply not possible.

Conclusion and recommendations

Reviewing the experiences of the three stakeholders indicates that there are real benefits to students, staff and entrepreneurs in terms of enhancing entrepreneurial knowledge, developing technical skills and increasing employability skills. The knowledge acquired in the creation of the wikis has demonstrated that wikis can offer an effective and efficient mechanism in the teaching, learning and assessment process and reinforces observations made previously. The experiences and output strengthens the potential of wikis as a collaborative learning tool to source and develop information, irrespective of time and place. The experiences of this iteration nonetheless reveal solutions need to be developed regarding group work, particularly when activities are not assessed. This issue is magnified when juxtaposed to the reality of other work and academic commitments that are assessable. It is evident, regrettably, that assessing an activity is often critical in driving and deepening the learning experience; however, by engaging in repeated reflective practices allowed the stakeholders to identify and resolve problems. This recourse sat well with the action learning approach taken and enjoyed support from the students, since it aligned to a key tenet of their programme. On reflection, other issues will need to be addressed, including how to develop relationships remotely, since the research team aims to continue building wiki projects in collaboration with commercial and not-for-profit organisations, which are not based locally. A further area of review will consider evaluating and developing the entrepreneurs' technical skills to ensure their confidence and ability in monitoring and assessing the wikis. The study highlighted the importance of involving everyone in the activity, suggesting a need to think further about entrepreneurial learning on a multifaceted level; student, nascent entrepreneur, entrepreneur and academic. The building block of reflective practice in entrepreneurial learning is centred on the activity and subsequent experiences of self and others. In terms of education practice and processes, wikis' role is still emerging; however, increasingly experience demonstrates and resonates with mainstream theory in seeking to explore the interplay of wikis, entrepreneurship education, learning and multiple stakeholders; which the research team believes can satisfy the needs and expectations of various educational stakeholders.

References

Anderson, A., & Jack, S. (2008). Role typologies for enterprising education: The professional artisan? *Journal of Small Business and Enterprise Development, 15*(2), 259–273.

Argyris, C., & Schön, D. (1974). *Theory in practice: Increasing professional Effectiveness.* San Francisco, CA: Jossey-Bass.

Bergh, P., Thorgren, S., & Wincent, J. (2011). Entrepreneurs learning together: The importance of building trust for learning and exploiting business opportunities. *International Entrepreneurial Management Journal, 7*, 17–37.

Borzsony, P., & Hunter, K. (1996). Becoming a learning organization through partnership. *The Learning Organization, 3*(1), 22–30.

Brunetto, Y., & Farr-Wharton, R. (2007). The moderating role of trust in SME owner/manager decision making about collaboration. *Journal of Small Business Management, 45*(3), 362–387.

Bumpus, M., & Burton, G. (2008). Chapters in the life of an entrepreneur: A case study. *Journal of Education for Business,* (7), 605–622.

Cambridge Report. (2007). *Looking inwards, reaching outwards. The Cambridge Cluster Report 2007.*Cambridge: Library House.

Chen, H., Cannon, D., Gabrio, J., Leifer, L., Toye, G., & Bailey, T. (2005). *Using wikis and weblogs to support reflective learning in an introductory engineering design course*. Proceedings of the 2005 American Society for Engineering Education, Annual Conference & Exposition, Portland, Oregon.

Cheng, Y.C. (2005). Development of multiple thinking and creativity in organizational learning. *International Journal of Educational Management, 19*(7), 605–622.

Chu, S. (2008). Twiki for knowledge building and management. *Online Information Review, 32*(6), 745–758.

Cole, M. (2008). Using wiki technology to support student engagement: Lessons from the trenches. *Computers & Education, 52*, 141–146.

Collins, L., Smith, A., & Hannon, P. (2006). Applying a synergistic learning approach in entrepreneurship education. *Management Education, 37*(3), 335–354.

Cope, J., & Watts, G. (2000). Learning by doing – an exploration of experience, critical incidents and reflection in entrepreneurial learning. *International Journal of Entrepreneurial Behaviour and Research, 6*(3), 104–124.

Cronin, J. (2009). Upgrading to Web 2.0: An experiential project to build a marketing wiki. *Journal of Marketing Education, 31*(1), 66–75.

Desmarais, L., Parent, R., Leclerc, L., Raymond, L., MacKinnon, S., & Vezina, N. (2008). Knowledge transfer between two geographically distant action research teams. *Journal of Workplace Learning, 21*(3), 219–239.

Dickens, L., & Watkins, K. (1999). Action research: rethinking Lewin. *Management Learning, 30*(2), 127–140.

Ecclestone, K. (2007). Commitment, compliance and comfort zones: The effects of formative assessment on vocational education students' learning careers. *Assessment in Education: Principles, Policy & Practice, 14*(3), 315–333.

Financial Services Skills Council. (2010). *The employability skills challenge: Research from the financial services and education sectors, June 2010*. Financial Services Skills Council.

Foss, L. (2010). Research on entrepreneur networks: The case for a constructionist feminist theory perspective. *International Journal of Gender and Entrepreneurship, 2*(1), 83–102.

Gibb, A. (1998). *Entrepreneurial core capacities, competitiveness and management development in 21st century*. Keynote address to the International Entrepreneurship Education Conference, Frankfurt, 1–21 June.

Hartshorne, R., & Ajjan, H. (2009). Examining student decisions to adopt Web 2.0 technologies: Theory and empirical tests. *Journal of Computing Higher Education, 21*, 183–198.

Halcro, K. (2008). *The influence of stakeholders upon the strategy of independent Scottish museums during the organisational life cycle*. PhD thesis, Queen Margaret University, Edinburgh.

Hatton, N., & Smith, D. (1995). Reflection in teacher education: Towards definition and implementation. *Teaching and Teacher Education, 11*(1), 33–49.

Hearn, G., Foth, M., & Gray, H. (2008). Applications and implementations of new media in corporate communications. *Corporate Communications: An International Journal, 14*(1), 49–61.

Hendrix, D. (2007). Focusing on behaviours and learning at Shell. *Knowledge Management Review, 10*(3), 8–13.

Huebscher, J., & Lendner, C. (2010). Effects of entrepreneurship simulation game seminars on entrepreneurs' and students' learning. *Journal of Small Business and Entrepreneurship, 23*(4), 543–554.

Husu, J., Toom, A., & Patrikainen, S. (2008). Guided reflection as a means to demonstrate and develop student teachers' reflective competencies. *Reflective Practice: International and Multidisciplinary Perspectives, 9*(1), 37–51.

Hyland, F., Trahar, S., Anderson, J., & Dickens, A. (2008). *A changing world the internationalisation experience of student and staff in UK higher education*. The Higher Education Academy.

Janasz, S., & Forret, M. (2007). Learning the art of networking a critical skill for enhancing social capital and career success. *Journal of Management Education, 20* (10), 1–21.

Jackson, P. (2010). Capturing, structuring and maintaining knowledge: A social software approach. *Industrial Management + Data Systems, 110*(6), 908–919.

Karabenick, S., & Knapp, J. (1991). Relationship of academic help seeking to the use of learning strategies and other instrumental achievement behavior in college students. *Journal of Educational Psychology, 83*(2), 221–230.

Kemmis, S., & McTaggart, R. (2000). Participatory action research. In N.K. Denzin & Y.S. Lincoln (Eds.), *Handbook of qualitative research* (2nd ed.) (pp. 567–605). Thousand Oaks, CA: Sage.

Klenowski, V., & Lunt, I. (2007). Enhancing learning at doctoral level through the use of Reflection. *Assessment and Evaluation in Higher Education, 33*(2), 203–217.

Kolb, D. (1984). *Experiential learning experience as a source of learning and development.* Englewood Cliffs, NJ: Prentice Hall.

Knowles, M. (2005). *The adult learner: The definitive classic in adult education and human resource development* (6th ed.). Burlington, MA: Elseiver.

Laff, M. (2007). The world according to wiki. *T+D, 61*(5), 28–31.

Levy, M., & Hadar, I. (2010). Teaching MBA students the use of Web 2.0: The knowledge management perspective. *Journal of Information systems Education, 21* (1), 55–67.

Ma, W., & Yuen, A. (2008). News writing using wiki: Impacts on learning experience of student journalists. *Educational Media International, 45*(4), 295–309.

Mann, K., Gordon, J., & MacLeod, A. (2009). Reflection and reflective practice in health professions education: A systematic review. *Advances in Health Science Education, 14*(4), 595–621.

McCarthy, J., Smith, J., & DeLuca, D. (2010). Using online discussion boards with large and small groups to enhance learning of assistive technology. *Journal of Computing Higher Education, 22*, 95–113.

McKelvie, G., Dotska, F., & Patrick, K. (2007). Interactive business development, capturing business knowledge and practice. *The Learning Organisation, 14*(5), 407–422.

McKiernan, G. (2005). Wikimedia worlds part 1: Wikipedia. *Library High Tech News, 8*, 46–54.

Minocha, S. (2009). Role of social software tools in education: A literature review. *Education + Training, 51*(5/6), 353–369.

Mlitwa, N. (2007). Technology for teaching and learning in higher education contexts: Activity theory and actor network analytical perspectives. *International Journal of Education and Development, 3*(4), 54–70.

Morrison, K. (1996). Developing reflective practice in higher degree students through a learning journal. *Studies in Higher Education, 21*(3), 317–332.

Mwasalwiba, E. (2010). Entrepreneurship education: A review of its objectives, teaching methods and impact indicators. *Education + Training, 52*(1), 20–47.

Ottewill, R. (2003). What's wrong with instrumental learning? The case of business and management *Education + Training, 45*(4), 189–196.

Pack, M. (2011). More than you know: Critically reflecting on learning experiences by attuning to 'community of learners'. *Reflective Practice, 12*(1), 115–125.

Pittaway, L., & Cope, J. (2007a). Entrepreneurship education: A systematic review of the evidence. *International Small Business Journal, 25*(5), 479–498.

Pittaway, L., & Cope, J. (2007b). Simulating experiential learning: Integrating experiential and collaborative approaches to learning. *Management Learning, 38*(2), 211–233.

Rae, D. (2000). Understanding entrepreneurial learning: A question of how? *International Journal of Entrepreneurial Behaviour and Research, 6*(3), 145–159.

Rae, D., & Carswell, M. (2000). Using a life-story approach in researching entrepreneurial learning: The development of a conceptual model and its implications in the design of learning experiences. *Education and Training, 42*(4/5), 220–228.

Raelin, J.A. (1999). The design of the action project in work–based learning. *Human Resource Planning, 22*(3), 12–28.

Rowley, T. (1997). Moving beyond dyadic ties: A network theory of stakeholder influences. *Academy of Management Review, 22*(4), 887–910.

Silverman, D. (2006). *Interpreting qualitative data: Methods for analyzing talk, text and interaction* (3rd ed.). London: Sage.

Smith, A., Halcro, K., & Chalmers, D. (2009). *Using Web 2.0 technology in entrepreneurship education: Wikis as a tool for collaborative and collective learning proceedings.* Paper presented at the 32nd ISBE Conference, Liverpool, 3–6 November.

Smith, A.M.J., & Paton, R. (2011). Delivering global enterprise: International and collaborative entrepreneurship in education. *International Journal of Entrepreneurial Behaviour & Research, 17*(1), 104–118.

Taylor, D., Jones, O., & Boles, K. (2004). Building social capital through action learning: An insight into the entrepreneur. *Education + Training, 46*(5), 226–235.

Tuckman, B. (1965). Development sequence in small groups. *Psychological Bulletin, 63*, 384–399.

Wheeler, S., Yeomans, P., & Wheeler, D. (2008). The good, the bad and the wiki: Evaluating student-generated content for collaborative learning. *British Journal of Educational Technology, 39*(6), 987–995.

Wood, A. (2010). Using emerging technologies to enhance learning. *Nursing Science Quarterly, 23*(2), 173–179.

Xiao, Q., Marino, L., & Zhuang, W. (2010). a situated perspective of entrepreneurial learning: Implications for entrepreneurial innovation propensity. *Journal of Business and Entrepreneurship, 22*(1), 69–89.

Index